# Primary Reading Skills Activities Kit

Elizabeth A. McAllister, Ed.D.

**THE CENTER FOR APPLIED
RESEARCH IN EDUCATION**
West Nyack, New York 10995

10   9   8   7   6   5   4   3   2   1

**Library of Congress Cataloging-in-Publication Data**

McAllister, Elizabeth A.
    Primary reading skills activities kit.

    Bibliography: p.
    1. Reading (Primary)   2. Activity programs in
education.   3. Creative activities and seatwork.
I. Title.
LB1525.M452   1987      372.4'1      87-24989


ISBN 0-87628-656-2

 **THE CENTER FOR APPLIED
RESEARCH IN EDUCATION**
BUSINESS & PROFESSIONAL DIVISION
A division of Simon & Schuster
West Nyack, New York 10995

Printed in the United States of America

## ACKNOWLEDGMENTS

From the inception of compiling knowledge and ideas in this manuscript, many others have influenced its completion. I would like to acknowledge those who deserve my thanks and appreciation. They are: the Great Educator from whom all ideas flow; my husband, Bob, for his love, confidence, and continual encouragement; Dr. Betty Anderson, friend, mentor, and colleague at the University of Central Florida in Orlando, Florida, who painstakingly read the entire original manuscript during its development and offered many suggestions and insights; and to my students and friends who have put many of these activities to the test in their classrooms, further fueling motivation for the task. And lastly, to my daughters, Debra, Sandra, and Rhonda, for their uplifting support, humor, patience, and understanding during this endeavor. To each of these, my love and indebtedness. Thanks!

E.A.M.

## ABOUT THE AUTHOR

Elizabeth McAllister, Ed.D. (University of Florida, Gainesville), has been involved in education for over seventeen years. She has served as a primary classroom teacher, reading specialist, and curriculum resource teacher, as well as an assistant professor at several colleges and universities in Florida and Tennessee.

Dr. McAllister is currently Associate Professor of Elementary Education at Tennessee Wesleyan College in Athens, Tennessee.

# ABOUT THIS KIT

*Primary Reading Skills Activities Kit* consists of over 140 activities that teach and reinforce specific pre-reading and beginning reading skills. The *Kit* has been developed to help you, the primary grade teacher, in recognizing and developing skills that assure each child's continuous reading progress. You can assign the activities as independent learning center projects, for paired work, small group, or whole class participation.

Complete with easy-to-follow directions for construction and use, the activities are organized into two parts: developing reading readiness and beginning reading.

Part One explains how pre-reading skills are developed in the first five years of a child's life. Included in Part One are the following skills:

- Oral Communication and Visual Recognition (color recognition, shape recognition, comparisons, position, names of objects, classification)
- Visual Perception (position-in-space, spatial relationship, figure-ground differentiation, perceptual constancy, visual-motor development)
- Auditory Perception (figure-ground perception, auditory discrimination, auditory sequencing and memory, auditory sound-blending)

Part Two of the *Kit* provides activities for helping students begin to read. The following skills are included:

- Basic Reading Skills (visual letter recognition, visual discrimination of words, auditory discrimination of words and sounds in words)
- Word Attack (phonics, structural analysis)
- Sight Word Recognition (instant sight vocabulary)
- Vocabulary and Comprehension (word meanings, sequence, following directions, recognizing main ideas, factual recall, skimming for information, fact versus fantasy, true versus false, drawing conclusions)

After each skill section you will find ready-to-use Progress Charts and Skills Checklists you can reproduce as many times as needed for your students. The illustrated Progress Charts can be used as pre- and posttests, and function as report forms for parents as well as motivational proof to the students that progress is being made. The Skills Checklists can serve as observational records of pupil progress for your files.

A special feature of *Primary Reading Skills Activities Kit* is the information given at the end of the book. Here you will find:

- a glossary of reading terms
- sample word lists
- sources for referrals and skills tests

*Primary Reading Skills Activities Kit* can help you provide the fun and variety of activities that motivate children to learn and practice essential skills. With its easy-to-use format, the *Kit* will be just as rewarding and fun for you, too!

Elizabeth McAllister

# HOW TO USE THIS KIT

Before planning your reading skills program, you need to find out what kind of verbal experiences the children in your class have had in the five years before you met them. Something has been going on in their environment. How richly that environment prepared each child may vary by a wide degree. The very expressive, quick-to-respond youngsters will stand out immediately. The completely non-verbal ones will also be very obvious. But the timid, sometimes-verbal children can be easily overlooked.

## OBSERVE AND CLASSIFY VERBAL ABILITY

A good way to start is by informally observing and grouping these children on a list by verbal, sometimes-verbal and non-verbal classification. Take the sometimes-verbal children aside and ask them questions about everyday things. You will immediately notice whether or not the child answers in complete sentences or just one- or two-word utterances or nods. Probably, you will want to split this group further so that the ones who can respond in complete sentences will group closer to the verbal children. The ones who answer in short, jerky utterances will group closer to the non-verbal children and will require more help.

## BE ALERT TO PHYSICAL AND ENVIRONMENTAL FACTORS

Success in learning to read is influenced by the child's ability to listen and speak when he or she enters school, to be visually perceptive of environmental surroundings, and to be healthy physically, intellectually, and emotionally.

### Physical Factors

There are many physical factors that can influence learning to read. Among the most important are visual acuity and auditory acuity.

*Visual acuity* merely means "sharpness of vision." Children are born farsighted, with eyes one-third the size of the adult's eye. Some children are fully developed visually by age six. Visual readiness may not be completely developed before the age of eight.

Some symptoms that will alert you to the possibility of a vision problem are as follows.

1. The child tends to rub the eyes.
2. Materials are held closer to the face than normal.
3. The head is thrust forward.
4. The child's body is rigid while looking at distant objects.
5. Excessive head movements are used.
6. The child frowns, blinks, or squints while reading.
7. The child tilts the head to one side.
8. Tension is exhibited.
9. The child has a short attention span to visual stimuli.
10. Lip reading and gutteral utterances are used during reading.

If any or several of these symptoms are apparent, a professional vision examination should be recommended to the child's parents.

*Auditory acuity,* which is "sharpness of hearing," is not fully developed until about seven and one-half years of age. You can conduct a good observational test with a loud ticking clock. A normal child can hear the ticking up to forty-eight feet away. If the sound is not heard within twenty feet, the child will most likely experience difficulty with speech and phonetic analysis. A professional hearing examination is advised if you note any of these symptoms of hearing problems.

1. The child is unable to speak at a normal age.
2. The child cups one ear when listening or turns the ear toward the speaker.
3. He or she is a mouth breather or complains of ringing sounds.
4. The child listens with tense or blank facial expression.
5. The speech of others seems to be heard but not understood.
6. Pronunciation is faulty.
7. The child fails to respond to or remember oral directions.
8. The child is inattentive and restless.

## Intellectual, Maturational, and Experiential Factors

*Intelligence* is generally considered as the inherited potential a child has for learning. It is developed by the experiences presented to the child.

*Maturation* is an orderly and sequential pattern of nervous system development. While the pattern is consistent, development occurs at different rates in each person. The child, as a rule, sits up before standing and crawls before walking, and so forth.

Children need appropriate environmental stimulation activities for basic learning skills to develop at an appropriate rate. Biology (which is inherited) provides the potential to learn but environment changes the potential into learned abilities.

*Experiences* in the environment help the young child to mature and develop those skills that constitute his or her mental age level. This is the level of development that a child has reached by a given time. A child who is five and one-half to six years of age is not necessarily mentally developed to a six-year mental age.

The young child needs to perceive law and order in his or her world. He or she must become assertive and feel successful. The home environment must provide security so that mental energy can be applied to learning. This environment must offer a calm assuring atmosphere in order for the child to be healthy emotionally.

## WHAT YOU CAN DO TO HELP

The lowest verbally expressive pupils may have had little, if any, verbal and responsive stimulation for the five years before entering school. These children will need a good deal of creative, active stimulation in order to close the experience gap.

They will not be self-directed when placed in a reading program. Their readiness program may last three-fourths to one full year before they will be "ready" for a formal reading program.

You cannot rush a child through the involvement activities that develop the basic oral skills necessary for him or her to handle graphic-symbolic language. One academic year is not enough time to fill in a gap of five years of inexperience, so don't knock yourself out trying. Give these children as much rich experience in language as you can. GET THEM READY to learn.

## Brighten the Classroom Setting

The first step is oral communication based on awareness of things seen and heard. Turn your entire classroom into an awareness experience. The able students will gain by this exposure, even though they will go ahead in a formal reading program shortly after the beginning of school.

## Establish Learning Groups

Use the information gained from the Progress Charts and observations to form teaching groups consisting of students having similar weaknesses. Ad hoc skill groups can also be formed to work with tutors.

## Assign Activities

Specific activities for each skill area are listed in the Table of Contents. Simply refer to the appropriate section when planning for specific skill development. Offer suggested activities until they can be accomplished by the pupils.

To assure that pupils practice skills that need reinforcement, assign the activities suggested by the Progress Charts and see that they are completed satisfactorily. If they are not, provide additional activities as practice in the areas of weakness. If these are met satisfactorily by some children but not by all, ask successful students to help those in need with the practice activities.

## Evaluate Progress

The Progress Charts and Skill Checklists can be used as observational pretests and posttests. The illustrations depict the activity that is to be mastered. The charts give no indication of failure. They represent developmental progress only and should not be assigned a grade or referred to in that manner.

When an activity that is presented to a child is not accomplished, check the box on the chart that indicates "Not Mastered." Then, after a few activities for that skill have been practiced, reevaluate the skill and check "In Progress" if improvement has occurred but further work is needed. Continue the process of practice and recheck until the skill is mastered. Then, check the "Mastered" box to indicate that the skill has been accomplished.

The Skills Checklists correlate with the Progress Charts and are to be used as a record of pupil progress for your files and as a means of reporting to other staff members. The information gained by the Progress Chart activities is to be transferred to the appropriate Skill Checklist.

## A Word About Testing

No specific tests need precede the use of this material. The Progress Charts provided in this kit can be used as diagnostic tests. Their use can provide clues that alert you to trouble in each area. Don't get bogged down with long detailed evaluation unless the child appears to be severely handicapped.

## HOW TO SCHEDULE A REGULAR READING PROGRAM

While these skill development activities can be used as individual assignments, forming small learning groups and planning a regular skill development program will broaden your teaching efficiency. Let's talk about how to incorporate these activities into a regular reading program.

An organization/management system, as shown here, is one effective way to implement these activities. The system is designed to meet every child "where he or she is" on an instructional level and to provide continuous individualized activities to assure growth.

The students may be taught a rotation plan to follow, using a color-coded chart on the wall. Assigned groups (referred to as orange group 1, red group 2, blue group 3, green group 4, purple group 5, and yellow group 6) would have color tags on desks at the beginning of the school year.

Six stations hold activities for each child to practice specific skills at an appointed time. The stations may consist of teacher (group instruction), puzzles, tracing, audio station (headsets), clay, and writing.

A suggested teacher's schedule plan is shown here. A copy should be made and kept in your planbook during instruction time.

The wall chart, which keeps the group rotation schedule visible to the children, is shown here. A kitchen timer can be used to signal when to move to the next station. As an added reminder, the clocks on the chart show the "time" the children stay at each station.

The shapes on the chart are made of construction paper cut in geometric forms in appropriate colors. Each child can locate his or her group color on the chart.

Large black posterboard shapes and numerals hang from the ceiling directly over each station. Dividers to separate stations are made by standing seamstress cutting boards between two tables. This is an inexpensive way to provide areas that limit distraction. Also, large refrigerator boxes with one side cut off make excellent paint stations. Three sides are left open so that the child can step inside. Painting paper is tacked to the insides of the boxes.

Each numbered station has teacher-made activities as well as commercial materials. Not everything will be put out at once. Only the special types of activities the children should be using for reinforcement each day are to be visible.

Try this model, then modify or adapt it to fit your own classroom needs.

| Station Time | 1 Teacher | 2 Puzzles | 3 Tracing | 4 Audio | 5 Clay | 6 Writing |
|---|---|---|---|---|---|---|
| 8:00–8:15 | Orange | Red | Blue | Green | Purple | Yellow |
| 8:15–8:30 | Red | Blue | Green | Purple | Yellow | Orange |
| 8:30–8:45 | Blue | Green | Purple | Yellow | Orange | Red |
| 8:45–9:00 | Green | Purple | Yellow | Orange | Red | Blue |
| 9:00–9:15 | Purple | Yellow | Orange | Red | Blue | Green |
| 9:15–9:30 | Yellow | Orange | Red | Blue | Green | Purple |

| TIME | ① | ② | ③ | ④ | ⑤ | ⑥ |
|---|---|---|---|---|---|---|
| | orange | red | blue | green | purple | yellow |
| | red | blue | green | purple | yellow | orange |
| | blue | green | purple | yellow | orange | red |
| | green | purple | yellow | orange | red | blue |
| | purple | yellow | orange | red | blue | green |
| | yellow | orange | red | blue | green | purple |

# HOW TO EXPAND YOUR TEACHING PERFORMANCE

## Involve Other Teachers

If your school has separate teachers for music, art, and physical education, ask them to use some of these activities during their instruction time. Any of the cutting, pasting, and drawing activities lend themselves to art expression. Rhythmic movements and command activities fit well to music. Also, many rhymes are in songs. Physical education period is an excellent time in your day to offer gross motor and balance activities.

## Use Parent Power in the Classroom

Have parent meetings in your room. Invite interested parents to observe and to help. PARENT POWER is great! Take time to explain to parents what is needed and how impossible it is for you to meet all children's individual needs on a one-to-one basis. If you have a class of twenty-five to thirty pupils, you will probably be able to find at least ten parents who would be willing to come into the classroom to help children once or twice a week, for one or two hours each time. Can you imagine what a difference two extra adults in a classroom of twenty-five to thirty pupils can make? You will wonder how you ever got along without their assistance! And the enthusiasm of your students and these parents will be a wonder to see.

Invite parents in on a rotation basis and ask them to oversee some of the learning activities you have planned for the school day. They can work with small groups of children, fifteen to thirty minutes daily, while you are teaching the curriculum.

## Plan for Parent Helpers

Write the names of the volunteer parents right in your planbook. Let them know they are an important part of your scheduling during the "reading" period. When parents realize that children are looking forward to a turn to work with "their parent," it stimulates interest and dependability.

You should do the actual planning and teaching. The parents will then work with a small group to see that instructions were understood, to help where help is needed, or just be verbally involved. This frees you to instruct other children without being interrupted.

## For Parents Who Are Homebound

Parents who are not able to attend during the day but would like to help can make games and manipulative activities for use in the classroom. You would provide the materials and instructions shown in the activities. Summer is a good time to get the needed materials ready. Then work on "coming events" as you progress through the school year. You will be amazed at how fast your supply of teaching materials will grow!

## Other Sources of Help

At the end of this *Kit* is a list of referral sources and alternative evaluation instruments that can be used if further diagnostic help is needed. The evaluative instruments suggested have been selected and tested for their ease of administration and interpretation.

# CONTENTS

## Appendix B   243

## Appendix C   249

# PART ONE

# Developing Reading Readiness

## CHAPTER ONE

# Building Basic Language Skills at Home

Every teacher of primary grade students has seen the frustration of children unable to make themselves understood. Many new students have had such a barren experience before entering school that they are overwhelmed by all of the sights and sounds that assail them in the classroom. Not only does the environment astonish and frighten them but, suddenly, a stranger is expecting them to respond to a specific question.

Many people mistakenly assume that learning a native language is an easy process. Often there is a lack of attention in the home paid to learning through example and practice, and a child's speaking accomplishments are taken for granted. However, the child's use of language is the key to future learning.

Through language, ideas and feelings are exchanged as a social process. Consistent characteristics of all language are that it is learned, it is made up of a code system and sequence of sounds, and it includes socially shared meanings.

The most important external factor affecting a child's rate of language development is the child's language environment at home for the five years before entering school. The child who lacks this early experience rarely catches up to children who come into the classroom verbally expressive. It is vital that you make this point known to the parents of your pupils. Each pupil must be able to express himself verbally in order to learn other communication skills such as reading and writing.

The five years of preschool experiences should afford each child opportunities to interact verbally within his environment. During these years, the child's vocabulary increases from just the few words of a one-year-old to the several thousand words auditorily (through hearing) recognized by the first grader.

There is a definite relationship between early development of oral language (speech and listening) and the written language skills (reading and writing). Man is the only animal with the intelligent language system of talking, reading, writing, and reasoning. Language brings about the greatest development of the human brain and adds to the capacity for further development and expansion of thought.

## THE PARENT AS THE FIRST TEACHER

The parent is the first teacher in a child's life. This period of vital training begins the first time a new baby is spoken to. Before the baby's eyes can focus, he or she is taking in a voice and turning the head to the direction of that sound in an active response.

By listening and watching examples at home, the young child learns many concepts that enable him to interpret his environment. But, to develop skills as well as ideas, the child has to participate and respond orally, either in question or statement form. By listening, speaking, and sharing ideas, his or her understanding and usage of language is being developed.

Without the use of oral expression, the child may be deficient in reading, because written visual symbols are simply "talk" put down on paper.

If a pupil has not been involved and accepted verbally long before coming to school, printed ideas will convey no message to him. Without ideas in his or her mind to conjure pictorial memory of what the word in print is saying, the pupil will not be able to remember the printed word forms.

## HOME BACKGROUND PREDICTS READING SUCCESS

There is a definite relationship between the use of language at home prior to entering school and reading achievement in first grade. High achieving readers come from enriched verbal environments where they have engaged in conversations with parents, have been exposed to books and have been read to frequently.

If a child is not spoken to daily, she will not learn to listen and carry out directions. She will not learn to watch, to be visually aware of surroundings, and to express verbally what she sees or hears. Ideas and understanding of words are internalized for future use every time a child is spoken to and every time he or she responds actively to what is seen or heard. This is what is meant by a healthy language environment.

Some parents are not aware of their vital function in developing readiness for learning, but most parents are interested in how they can help in their children's education. It is up to you to show parents how to help and to stress the important difference they can make between having a reader and a nonreader in the primary grades.

## ACTIVITIES THAT BUILD BASIC LANGUAGE SKILLS

Following is a list of activities that you can share with parents for the development of basic visual/auditory/oral skills and concepts that prepare a child to listen, concentrate, and use their ears and eyes as a means of getting information and learning in school.

1. *Point To:* Concepts such as naming objects, color, sizes, and comparisons can be stressed with this activity.

    a. *Naming*
    Ask the child to point to the window, sink, table, chair, and other objects around the house.

    b. *Discriminating*
    Have the child point to the red socks on the clothesline, the green glass on the shelf, the blue bird in the tree, and so forth.

    c. *Size comparison*
    Tell the child to point to the big chair, the little toy, the smallest shoes, the largest person.

2. *Bring Me:* This is good for training students to listen to directions and follow through with responses. Start simply with only one idea to be remembered and gradually add commands.

    a. *One object*
    In oral commands, have the child bring a cup, towel, book, or the like. This is only one object to be remembered at a time.

    b. *Two ideas, one object*
    Have the child bring the green towel, yellow soap, or loaf of bread. These offer two ideas to remember through the action even though there is only one object.

    c. *Object and location*
    Ask the child to bring the can of beans from the cupboard. This is expanding the concept to include an object in a particular location.

    d. *Three ideas*
    Use commands including where to go, what to find, and where to find the object. For example: Bring the green towel hanging on the towel bar in the bathroom.

    e. *Four-step directions*
    Ask the child to go to the bedroom, open the underwear drawer, pick out a pair of blue socks, and bring them to you. Have the child repeat all four steps verbally before attempting to carry them through.

These sorts of commands train the young student to listen, think, compare, and reason. Each activity should start simply and always follow through with examples when uncertainty is shown. The child should be equally involved verbally as the commands are being carried out.

3. *Show Me:* In this activity use as many common descriptive words as possible.

    a. Have the child show you something big, yellow, heavy, pretty, round, square, and so forth.

b. Use picture books to develop descriptive concepts. Look for pictures of a happy face, a sad face, or someone running, reading, or eating. Have the child describe what he sees in each picture.

4. *"Reading" Together*

a. Nursery rhymes should be read aloud and recited any time, anywhere, until the child can do this independently.

b. Have books around the house with large pictures to be looked at and wondered about. Ask the child what is happening in the pictures, how he would feel if he were there.

c. Have the child describe the picture. Ask questions about who is in the picture, where the picture is made (outside, inside, under the table), what is happening, why the animals are smiling, why the boy is crying, and so on. This type of questioning is excellent for developing thought processes, looking for details, making up stories from pictures, and drawing conclusions.

d. Read short stories to the child. Have him or her retell the story by asking who, where, when, and what happened questions. If these questions cannot be answered, reread that part of the story and then repeat the questions.

5. *I Wonder What Then:* Use ideas the child understands in this activity. State the "way it is" and ask how different it would be if things were changed.

a. "I wonder if you would know when to sleep if the clock were broken." Let the child respond.

b. "I wonder what you would do for milk if there were no more cows." Let the child respond.

c. After watching television, ask the child what he thinks will happen next or what happened before the incident.

6. *Let's Take A Walk:* During a walk around the block, many concepts can be observed and discussed.

a. Start by looking for a specific thing. Tell the child to look for blades of grass, tree leaves, bushes, and the like. Look closely and compare how they are alike and different.

b. Flowers are a good example to use in color recognition. It is not intended for the child to memorize color words but to use colors as a discrimination tool. Simply make the child aware of color names of what he sees: the red roses, the yellow daffodils, the green grass, and so forth.

c. Size comparison can be utilized during a walk. Look for the largest house, the smallest house, and the tallest tree.

d. Clouds are fun to watch and discuss because their traits and characteristics change. Ask the child what he sees in the clouds.

e. Walk in light rain one day. It is quite an experience! Have the child discuss how it feels, looks, tastes, and smells. Discuss whether it is cold, hot, dry, or wet. Does the grass drink it?

7. Let the young child help sort clothes. He or she can group items into piles of underwear, towels, washcloths, and so forth. He is starting to develop a mental image of organization.

8. Setting the table is a good exercise in directionality and placement in space. Discuss how many places are needed. Verbalize on which side of the plate the forks and knives are placed.

9. Let the child pair socks and organize them by colors even though the shades of color vary.

10. Have the child compare outside colors with the colors of clothes.

These are activities that certainly can be expanded. You can add other ideas to foster thinking, imagining, exploring, and verbalizing. Remember, readiness to learn is helped by the child's ability to visually discriminate and verbalize concepts about colors, sizes, positions of objects in relation to himself or herself, and similarities and differences. Be sure parents know how to help! Their help is healthy and educationally sound. Capitalize on the specific environment of your area: give specific suggestions involving local parks, exhibits, city and library facilities, stores, zoos, and so on.

## CHAPTER TWO

# Building Oral Communication Skills and Visual Recognition

Each child needs to master certain basic oral concepts before he starts reading instruction. You will note that the involvement activities for parents to use at home include these concepts. Classroom activities can offer specific ways of expanding the same concepts and eliciting oral involvement during the school day.

You will want to have "whole group" involvement in each concept and skill before the children are asked to do independent activities at learning stations. Don't overlook this important step.

## THE IMPORTANCE OF THE SKILLS

The most basic ideas are color names and recognition, basic shape names and recognition, comparisons of likeness and size, positional words, names of objects, and classification. Each area will be discussed separately.

### Color Recognition

You will be surprised at how many children come to school not knowing colors or knowing color names. This does not mean just memorization of color words, but useful discrimination. Start each day by asking the color of Mary's dress or Jim's shirt. Who else is wearing the same color? When they are on the playground, ask the children to look for specific colors. Use every minute of the day for some development. There is never enough time.

## Shape Recognition

The most important factor of basic shapes is that they are so useful in comparison training, perceptual skills, and visual recognition of constancy between objects. The child uses so many of the line placements of basic shapes in forming letters that he or she needs to see this similarity. The shapes used are circle, square, rectangle, and triangle. Their use in perceptual training will be discussed further in the section on *Visual Perception*.

## Comparison Concepts

It is very important for the child to have a usable idea of big versus small and of sameness versus difference. Again, frequent "comparisons talk" makes every child sit up and notice examples. In class students can find all of the children with blue eyes or brown eyes, for an example of sameness. Line up three blue-eyed children and one brown-eyed child. Which one has eyes of a different color? Outside, which flowers are alike or different? Have the pupils verbally express the ideas with you. They need to HEAR whole ideas expressed to pick up language form. Any two or more objects or children can be compared in this way daily. The idea must be kept verbally in front of the children all of the time. There can't be too much interaction conversation.

## Positional Concepts

Before a child can learn which way to hold a book, he must know, understand, and be able to use positional words. For example: top/bottom, over/under, in/out, and left/right. Writing will be influenced by this concept. How else will a child understand that the stem is written below the line for a small "p" and above the line for other letters? Also, that the circle is to the "right" of the stem when writing a "b" and to the "left" of the stem when writing the letter "d."

## Names of Objects

Knowing and using names of objects assigns word labels to familiar concrete ideas. If the young pupil knows a "ball" is a ball, the word ball will make more sense in print.

## Classification

The ability to classify objects takes recognizing and naming a step further. To classify, the child must recognize attributes of each object that are similar in appearance, function, or quantity. This requires organizing learning content and fitting new content into an existing mental framework.

## MATERIALS TO GATHER

File folders

Shoe boxes

Construction paper, assorted colors

Marking pens (NON-TOXIC), assorted colors

Brads

Scissors

Glue

Catalogues and magazines

Pipe cleaners

Index cards, 3″×5″

Posterboard, assorted colors

Clay

Nails

Clothesline

Rag doll

Assorted clothes, two each (gloves, hats, shoes, socks, shirts, pants)

Small scarf boxes

Large box

Hula Hoop

Red plastic tape

Bulletin board paper, blue

Yarn

Dowels, ¼″×10″

Cardboard

Waxed paper

Dried beans

Paper dolls

Play telephones, two

Assorted small objects (toy furniture, tent, trash can, chair, table)

Animal Rummy cards

One-half pint milk cartons

Large manila envelopes

## ACTIVITIES THAT BUILD ORAL COMMUNICATION AND VISUAL RECOGNITION

The activities in this chapter are grouped under the headings of the basic concepts. Keep the flow of oral interaction going until you are sure that the concepts are understood by each student and useful to him or her.

Materials:          File folders
                    Colored construction paper, assorted
                    Marking pens, assorted
                    Scissors
                    Glue

Construction:       Line off both sides of a file folder so that there are 14
                    squares. Cut two 2″ circles out of each color of
                    construction paper. In every other square glue one of each
                    colored circle. Save the second copy in a pocket for
                    matching.

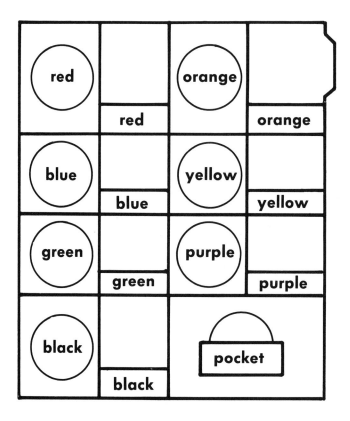

Activity:           The pupil removes the colored circles from the attached
                    pocket. Each color is matched by placing the same colored
                    circles in the boxes to the right of each color on the folder.

2-2. Color-Word Tree Bulletin Board Game          *Color Recognition*

Materials:              Green and brown construction paper
                        Blue bulletin board paper

Construction:           On a blue bulletin board staple a tree made of brown
                        paper (trunk and branches) with green foliage. Write a
                        color word on each branch.

Activity:               The pupils look for pictures of colored objects to tack onto
                        the branches of the color words.

Materials:        Blue bulletin board used in 2-2, with tree
                  Assorted colored construction paper
                  Scissors
                  Tacks

Construction:     Beneath the color-word tree, place stems. Cut a petal
                  pattern for each child. Give each student assorted colored
                  paper and pattern pieces.

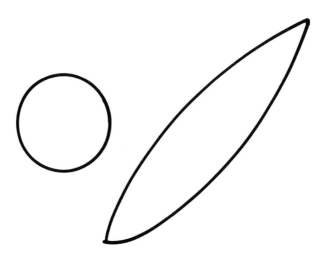

Activity:         The pupils cut petals out of assorted colored paper and
                  write the color name on each petal. Then, the "flowers"
                  are attached to the stems beneath the color-word tree.

**14**

Materials:            Posterboard, white
                      Assorted construction paper, 1″×2″
                      Assorted marking pens
                      Yarn

Construction:         Paste color strips on both sides of one board, and on the
                      left side of another board. With marking pens, write the
                      color names on the right side (red in red ink; blue in blue
                      ink, etc.). On the third board, paste color strips and write
                      the color names in black pen. Cut slits on both sides and
                      attach yarn for matching.

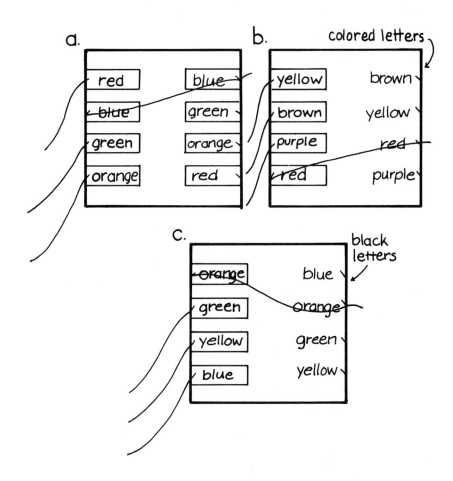

Activity:             a. Pupils match the same colored strips.
                      b. Pupils match color strips to color words written in the
                         appropriate colors.
                      c. Pupils match color strips to color words written in
                         black letters.

**15**

Materials:          White posterboard strips, $2'' \times 4''$
                    Assorted colored construction paper
                    Marking pen, black
                    Scissors
                    Glue

Construction:       Glue two different colors of 2″ squares to each side of the
                    $2'' \times 4''$ strips. On the *back side* write color words in each
                    square.

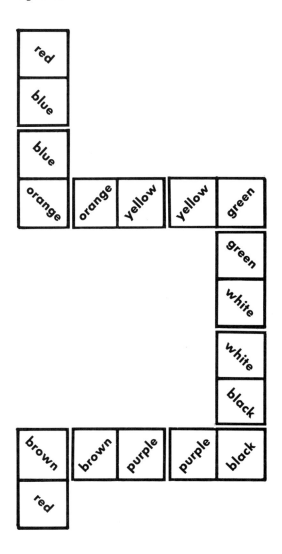

Activity:           Pupils lay color strips together to match the same colors
                    in a domino-type game. Later, the color word side is used
                    to match with the correct colors.

Materials:        Posterboard, white
                  Construction paper, assorted
                  Scissors
                  Glue
                  Yarn

Construction:     Cut and paste colored shapes on both sides of a 9″ × 12″
                  board. Cut slits in each side and insert yarn for
                  matching. On one board, paste two different sizes of each
                  shape.

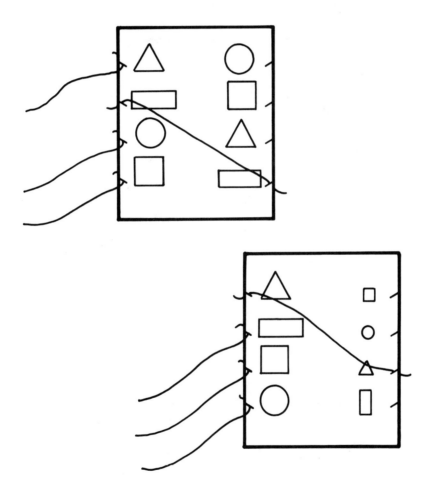

Activity:         a. Pupils match the same colored shapes.
                  b. Pupils match the same sized shapes, regardless of
                     color.
                  c. Pupils match the same shape, regardless of size
                     difference.

**17**

Materials:        Flannel squares, 9″ × 12″
Yarn
Patterns of shapes

Construction:     Make patterns of each shape for each child to have a
copy. Provide a flannel square 9″ × 12″ and yarn pieces.

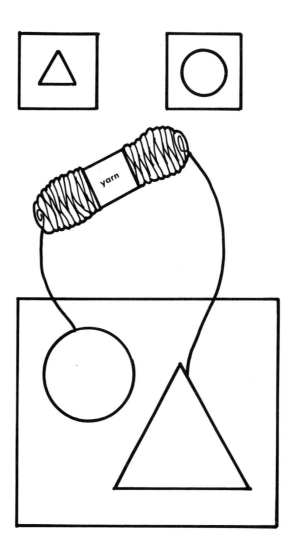

Activity:         The teacher holds up a shape card and has the children
"draw the shape" in the air. Then each child gets his or
her copy card and traces the outline of the shape. Next,
he or she uses a piece of yarn to make the same shape on
a piece of flannel.

Materials:            White posterboard pieces, 6″ × 6″
                      3″ × 5″ index cards
                      Marking pens
                      Dry lima beans

Construction:         Make bingo-type cards, for each child, showing shapes
                      drawn in a different position. On 3″ × 5″ cards draw
                      shape patterns with arrows to designate the right side
                      up.

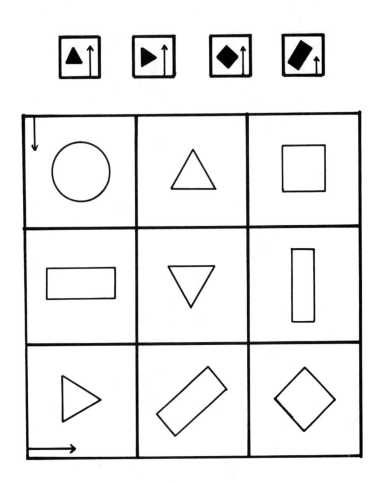

Activity:             Each pupil is given a bingo card and beans. You show a
                      shape and the child lays the bean on the same shape
                      shown on the card. The shape covered must be turned in
                      the same direction as the pattern card.

**19**

Materials:          White poster board, 10″ × 10″
                    Construction paper, assorted
                    Dry lima beans
                    3″ × 5″ index cards

Construction:       Square off five lines in both directions on 10″ × 10″
                    posterboard. In each square paste shapes of different
                    colors. Make pattern cards of the same colored shapes.

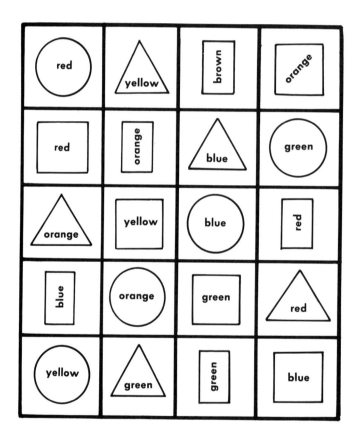

Activity:           Give each pupil a bingo card and beans. You hold up the
                    colored shape patterns. The pupils cover the correct
                    shape in a specific color.

**20**

Materials:          Clothesline
                    Nails
                    Construction paper, assorted colors
                    Clothespins

Construction:       Cut two copies of each object of clothing. Nail a
                    clothesline beneath the chalkboard or bulletin board.

Activity:           The pupils match the SAME colors and clothes by
                    pinning them together on the clothesline.

Materials:        Box of assorted objects
Tagboard, 12″×18″
Marking pens

Construction:    Cut tagboard strips 18″×4″. On each strip write in large letters the size concept words (short, tall, big, small) you are stressing. Place two or three of each object (different in size or color) in a large box.

Activity:         A child pulls out two items and describes them. Other children add additional description denoting size, color, sameness, or difference. You make word cards of the descriptive words and display them on a wall. Later, during activities with other objects, refer to these word cards and concepts.

2-12. Which Is Different?                    *Comparison Concepts*

Materials:          Long file folders
                    Brads
                    Tagboard
                    Marking pens, assorted

Construction:       Line off six rows. Draw four pictures, three alike and one
                    different, on each row. Attach an arrow with a brad to
                    each row center.

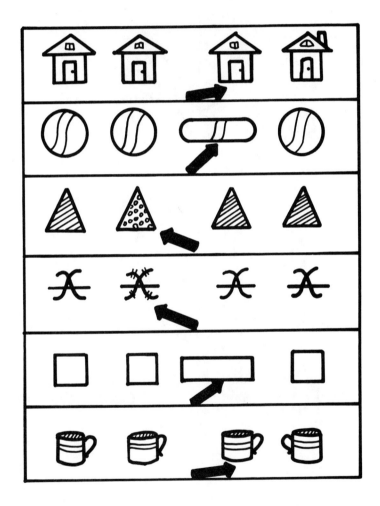

Activity:           The pupil moves the arrow on each row to point to the
                    picture that is different.

Materials: Small bulletin board
Blue bulletin board paper
Construction paper, assorted
Scissors
Stapler

Construction: On a blue bulletin board, place free-form cut flowers on stems. Make many different kinds, sizes, and colors.

Activity: Take a group of children to the bulletin board. Point to specific flowers and have the children describe and compare the flowers using shape, size, and color concepts.

2-14. Top/Bottom; Up/Down *Positional Concepts*

**Materials:**    Masking tape
Marking pens, red and black
Objects; such as, shoe, toy tent, toy furniture, trash can,
chair, table, desk, and the like

**Construction:**    On each object, place two strips of masking tape; one on
top and one on bottom. On the top tape write the word
*top* in black letters. On the bottom tape write the word
*bottom.* Place a third tape vertically on the side of each
object. In red, draw an arrow and write *up* at the top of
the arrow and *down* at the bottom of the arrow.

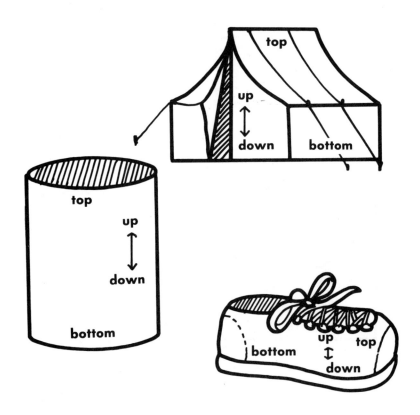

**Activity:**    The pupil removes the object and tells the class or group
which is the top or bottom of each object. Then, he or she
shows the arrow depicting the up and down directions.
Let each child bring in an additional object for sharing.

**25**

Materials:        Tagboard
Scissors
Overhead projector
Small objects: buttons, rubber bands, paper clips, or brads

Construction:      Cut out two tagboard shapes for each child. Also, supply other loose objects for demonstration purposes.

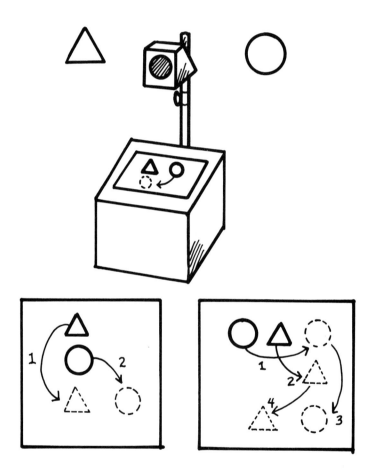

Activity:        Before the pupils begin, use the small objects on an overhead projector. Move objects around, discussing the change in position each time. For example: The paper clip is being moved over, under, or to the left or right of the button. Then, give each child two shapes. Use the same two shapes on the overhead, having the pupils move their pieces with you while repeating each directional move.

Materials:              Large box
                        Hula Hoop or rope
                        Red tape
                        Chair

Construction:           None. Just place red tape on the Hula Hoop, box, and
                        chair to denote the "front" of each object.

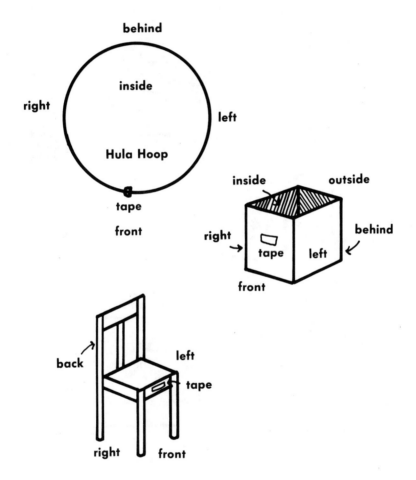

Activity:               Select three children at a time. Place the Hula Hoop, box,
                        and chair in front of the room. Stand a child in *front* of
                        the red tape on each object. Give oral directions for the
                        children to move behind, in back of, in front of, inside, on,
                        outside, to the left, or to the right of each object.

27

Materials: Posterboard
Pictures of birds
Marking pens, assorted

Construction: On the posterboard, draw three birdhouses. Glue birds in different locations on the board. Write positional words on cards. Place these beneath each bird.

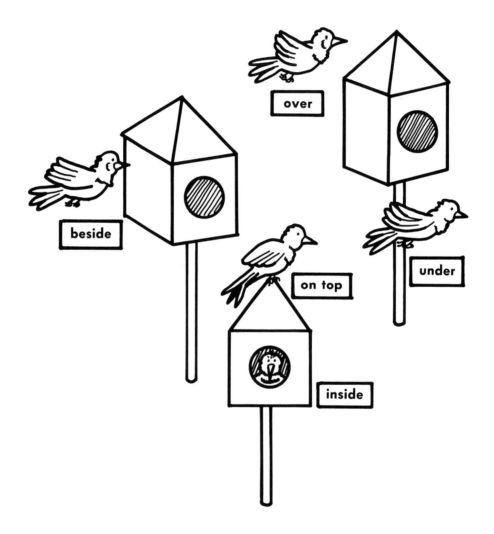

Activity: Involve children in discussion about the location of each bird. Example: Find the bird that is "over," "on top of," "inside," "under," or "beside" a birdhouse.

Materials:           Magazines or catalogues
                     Posterboard
                     Marking pens
                     Scissors
                     Glue

Construction:        Cut large, clear pictures out of magazines and glue them
                     onto 5″ × 7″ posterboard. Write the picture name beneath
                     each picture and cut zigzag through both name and
                     picture.

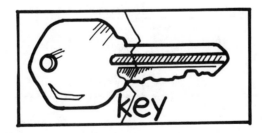

Activity:            The pupils put the pictures together in a puzzle-type
                     activity that also gives practice in completion of letters
                     and words.

*Names of Objects*

Materials:        Shoe boxes
                  Marking pens
                  Small miscellaneous objects as shown

Construction:     Square off the lids and bottoms of the boxes. In each
                  square, write the name of the objects that are contained
                  in that box. Small objects from gum machines, games,
                  toys, and tiny doll clothes can be used.

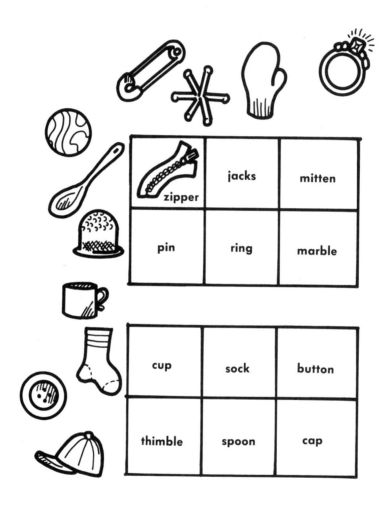

Activity:         The pupil removes the objects from the box. He or she
                  then places each object in the square that contains the
                  object's name.

Materials:           Posterboard, 6″ × 6″ (4 or 6 pieces)
                                 Marking pens
                                 Catalogues

Construction:      Line off two-inch squares. Draw or paste pictures in each square. Make word cards for each picture.

Activity:          This game is played like bingo, using the word cards. Word cards are held up and read to the children. The pupils cover the picture that the card names.

31

Materials:            Construction paper, two colors
                      Catalogues
                      Marking pens
                      Scissors
                      Glue

Construction:         Cut cards 2½″ × 3″ (equal number of each color). On one
                      deck glue pictures. On the second deck, write the word
                      naming each picture and draw an outline of its shape.

Activity:             Deal the picture cards. The pupils draw from the word
                      deck. Players who have the correct picture and can name
                      it keep both cards.

2-22. Bird, Animal, or Fish?                    *Classification*

Materials:          Commercial card game of Animal Rummy
                    Small box with lid
                    Marking pen

Construction:       Draw three sections in the bottom of the box. Write the
                    words *birds, animals,* and *fish* in the sections. Glue a
                    pocket in the lid and one picture in each section.

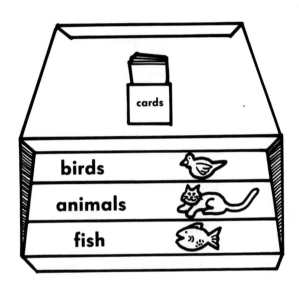

Activity:           Pupils remove the entire deck of cards. They are to be
                    sorted and each card is to be placed in the correct section
                    naming the category of the picture.

Materials:      Heavy cardboard
Small half-pint milk cartons
Construction paper
Assorted nails
Cellophane tape
Glue
Scissors
Staples

Construction:      Wash the cartons and cut off their tops. Staple the backs to a piece of heavy cardboard. Cut pails out of construction paper and glue these to the front of each box. Tape one nail to each pail. Place one pail box in the lower right corner for storage.

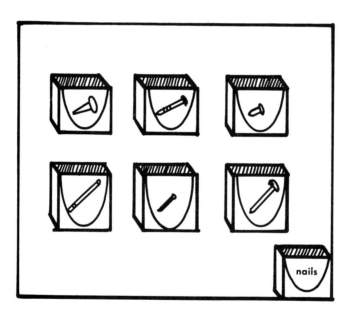

Activity:      Pupils remove nails one at a time and place each one in the corresponding nail pail.

2-24. Where Does It Belong?                               *Classification*

Materials:          Large brown envelopes
                    Small letter envelopes
                    Catalogues
                    Scissors
                    Construction paper
                    Marking pens

Construction:       Choose three topics for classification, such as furniture,
                    clothes, and utensils. Cut out pictures of items that fit
                    into each of these categories. Glue these to 3″ × 3″ cards of
                    construction paper. Under each picture write the item's
                    name. Make a construction paper card 8″ × 9″, divide it
                    into squares, and write item names in each square as
                    shown. Glue small envelopes to the front of the large
                    brown envelope. On each envelope write the category
                    topics.

Activity:           The small pictures are matched to the category by
                    placing them in the correct small envelope. Also, the
                    pictures may be matched to the words on the large
                    construction paper card.

Materials:       One shallow scarf box
Assorted construction paper
Marking pens
Scissors
Glue

Construction:     Cut shapes from assorted colors. In a box lid, square off and paste one shape in each square. Write the color word beneath each shape in letters of the same color. The box bottom will contain black outlines and letters. Place loose cut shapes in the box for matching and color discrimination.

lid
colored shapes
and letters

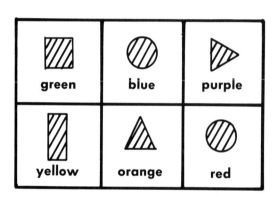

bottom
black outlined
shapes and
letters

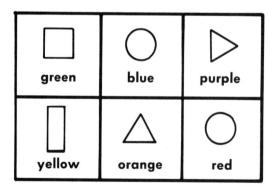

Activity:       a. Pupils match exact shape and color on the samples in the lid.
b. Pupils read color words and lay the correct colored shape on the outlines in the box. The lid can be used to check when the child cannot decide.

36

Name _____

Date _____

Progress Chart

## ORAL COMMUNICATIONS SKILLS and VISUAL RECOGNITION

Not Mastered/In Progress/Mastered

| | | |
|---|---|---|
| | | |

I can recognize and name colors.

Not Mastered/In Progress/Mastered

| | | |
|---|---|---|
| | | |

I can listen and follow directions.

Not Mastered/In Progress/Mastered

| | | |
|---|---|---|
| | | |

I express myself in complete sentences.

Name _____

Date _____

Progress Chart

# ORAL COMMUNICATIONS SKILLS and VISUAL RECOGNITION
## (continued)

Not Mastered/In Progress/Mastered

| | | |
|---|---|---|
| | | |

I understand and use positional words: up, down; over, under; and the like.

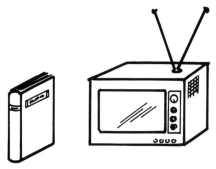

Not Mastered/In Progress/Mastered

| | | |
|---|---|---|
| | | |

I can name objects in my home.

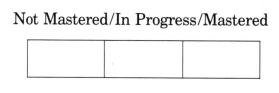

Not Mastered/In Progress/Mastered

| | | |
|---|---|---|
| | | |

I can describe what I see.

Name _____

Date _____

Progress Chart

## ORAL COMMUNICATIONS SKILLS and VISUAL RECOGNITION
### (continued)

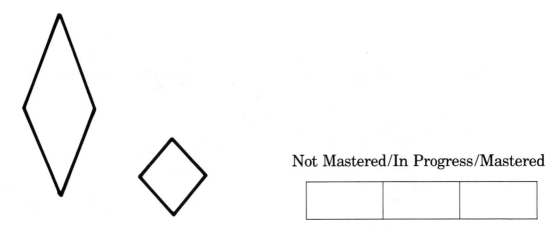

Not Mastered/In Progress/Mastered

| | | |
|---|---|---|
| | | |

I can recognize similarities and differences in shapes and sizes.

Not Mastered/In Progress/Mastered

| | | |
|---|---|---|
| | | |

I recognize things that are the same.

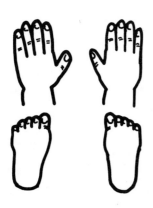

Not Mastered/In Progress/Mastered

| | | |
|---|---|---|
| | | |

I can name body parts and my left and right sides.

Name _____

Date _____

## ORAL COMMUNICATIONS SKILLS and VISUAL RECOGNITION
### (continued)

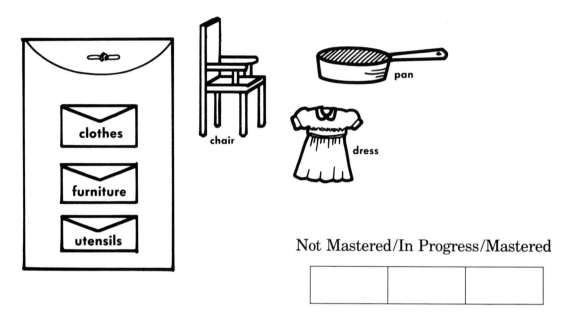

Not Mastered/In Progress/Mastered

|  |  |  |
|--|--|--|
|  |  |  |

I can classify objects.

Name _____

Date _____

## ORAL COMMUNICATIONS and
## VISUAL RECOGNITION SKILLS CHECKLIST

1. Recognizes and names colors. _____

2. Listens and follows directions. _____

3. Expresses himself or herself in complete
   sentences. _____

4. Understands and uses positional words. _____

5. Names common objects. _____

6. Describes what is seen. _____

7. Recognizes similarities and differences
   in shapes and sizes. _____

8. Recognizes things that are the same. _____

9. Names body parts and left and right sides
   of the body. _____

10. Classifies objects. _____

| Key: | ✔ Skill mastered |
|---|---|
| | X Needs further instruction |

## CHAPTER THREE

# Building Visual Perception Skills

From birth on, a young child has limited ability to discriminate (notice similarities and differences) and recognize stimuli (objects or sounds) in the environment. During infancy, he or she learns to interpret, adapt, and understand through the use of the senses and movement exploration.

Between the ages of three-and-a-half and seven-and-a-half, the discrimination abilities should sharpen. Now the eyes (looking) and ears (listening) become the most important channels of gaining knowledge.

The interpretation of what one sees or hears, based on using past experiences and memory, is called perception. All consciousness involves perception. Without perception, a human being cannot receive messages from the environment and respond to them. The enjoyment of what surrounds us in everyday life depends on refinement of perception . . . visual, auditory, kinesthetic (movement), and tactile (touch).

Visual perception is the primary channel through which we learn. Eighty percent of our perceptions are visual and eighty percent of all school work is acquired through the printed page.

Based on these facts alone, it is simply a matter of common sense to make certain that a child's visual perceptual skills are consciously fostered and developed. These interpretation skills can be trained and refined. Although improving perceptual skills does not teach skills of reading, strengthening perceptual weaknesses can remove major stumbling blocks in the process of learning to read. Why make a child scale a wall when he or she can walk up the steps to learning and enjoy the experience?

As the body is an organization of several parts, so is visual perception. Visual perception consists of five areas, each important to the wholeness of learning. These five areas are: position-in-space perception, spatial relationship perception, figure-ground differentiation, perceptual constancy, and visual-motor development. Perhaps only one area will be underdeveloped. That one weakness is enough to cause trouble when the pupil must interpret the printed page.

This chapter will give you information about each visual perception skill, its importance for reading success, and symptoms that interfere with learning. Training activities that you can easily develop, along with pupil progress charts and skills checklists, will be included.

## PERCEIVING POSITION IN SPACE

Probably, the first perceptual area to begin development is position-in-space perception. This is the perception (interpretation) of the relationship of an object to the observer.

## THE IMPORTANCE OF THE SKILL

There are prerequisites to this skill. Spatially, the young child is the center of his or her own world. Objects are perceived as being behind, before, above or below, or to his or her side. The interpretation of the child's own position in space is dependent on concept of self (the child's feeling of personal worth). He or she must first develop *body awareness* (knowledge of the body itself). This awareness is composed of three elements: body image, body concept, and body schema, in that order. These are the prerequisites to becoming spatially oriented.

*Body image* is the child's "feeling" of his or her own image. Has the child been spoken of as an attractive, likeable child? Or, has he or she been belittled and "made fun of" at home? The child's image is not necessarily expressed in movements; but can be best understood by drawings made by this child.

Then, *body concept* develops. This is the intellectual knowledge of one's body. It is acquired through *conscious learning* and through *verbalizing* that there are two arms, two legs, two eyes, two ears, hands on the arms, and feet on the legs, and, that the nose is in the *center* of the face and so forth. Then, *laterality* (knowledge of the left and right sides of the body) can be learned.

The last level of body awareness development is *body schema* (the unconscious idea of the body). It changes as the body uses different muscles and moves. Balance, maintaining equilibrium, and coordination depend on body schema development.

The child's ability to coordinate the eye and hand movements and to interpret position in space and spatial relationships depend on his or her body image, concept, and schema development. Also, after those three areas are developed, *directionality* (knowledge of left and right *in space*) can be learned.

A child must be able to function within space and time. A disability in position-in-space perception causes the child's visual world to become distorted. He or she is clumsy and hesitant in movements and has difficulty understanding what is meant by words designating his or her spatial position in relation to objects; such as in/out, up/down, before/behind, and left/right.

This skill is important to reading. Without it, the child cannot differentiate between the letters *b* and *d, p* and *q,* and words such as *on* and *no,* or *was* and *saw.*

Directionality weaknesses also effect reading. Without knowledge of left and right in space, the child may start from the right side of the page and read to the left; thus, causing reversals in reading. He or she may read *saw* for *was.* Also, the pupil may write backwards and exhibit problems of spacing within lines.

## MATERIALS TO GATHER

| | |
|---|---|
| Classroom furniture | Wooden counting blocks; 12 yellow, 12 red |
| Rope | |
| Construction paper, assorted colors | Spoons |
| | Cups |
| Scissors | Felt |
| Stapler | Marking pens, assorted |
| Glue | Manila paper |
| Bulletin board | Tagboard basic shapes |
| Bulletin board paper | Crayons |
| Magazines | Masking tape |

## ACTIVITIES THAT BUILD POSITION-IN-SPACE PERCEPTION

The following activities will help develop your student's position-in-space perception. Be sure that each student understands the concept.

Materials:       None

Construction:    None

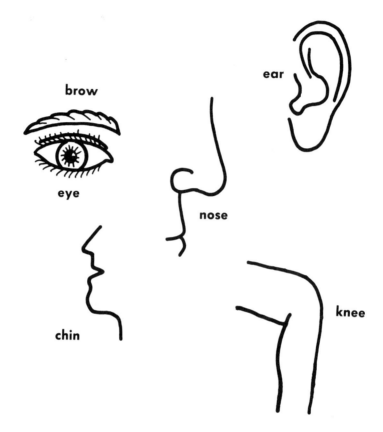

Activity:        With a group of children in front of the class, give verbal
commands for location and identification of body parts.
a. "With your hands, show me your ears, eyes, legs, feet,
shoulders."
The teacher touches parts and the pupils verbalize in
complete sentences.
b. "You touched my nose, chin, head, back, or ear."

3-2. Is It Left or Right?                                    *Position-in-Space*

Materials:        None

Construction:     None. Move desks aside or go outdoors.

Activity:         Two pupils are used as models, facing the same direction
                  as the class. Children stand an arm's length apart. The
                  teacher gives commands to move right or left arms, legs,
                  or hands, or to touch a particular body part. Pupils carry
                  out commands while naming the part indicated.

**47**

Materials:        None

Construction:     Remove furniture to make room for the children to change positions according to the model.

Activity:         Position a child in front of the class and have other children try to move into the same position as the model. Discuss which arm is forward, which leg is to the side.

Materials:          None

Construction:       None

"Lay on your stomach, raise up on your elbows, hold your chin with your left arm, bend your left knee to raise your left foot."

"Kneel on your knees and slant or lean back. Raise your arms to the front as though you are reaching for something."

Activity:           Give oral directions that describe exact movements and positioning. Have the children carry out the movements while verbalizing the sequence of action.

**49**

Materials:        Manila paper, $12'' \times 18''$
                  Tagboard basic shape templates
                  Marking pens
                  Red crayon

Construction:     On each sheet of manila paper, draw traffic lights in each
                  top corner. The left light should be colored green; the right
                  light, red (green for go and red for stop). Place an arrow
                  indicating a left-to-right direction at the top left corner.

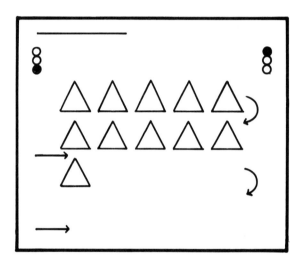

Activity:         Supply each pupil with shape templates, a manila page,
                  and a red crayon. Starting at the green light, the pupils
                  are to trace a row of shapes to the right. When the draw-
                  ings reach the red light, return to the green light and
                  trace another row. Continue until the page is full of
                  shapes.

Name _____

Date _____

## Progress Chart

### POSITION-IN-SPACE PERCEPTION

Not Mastered/In Progress/Mastered

| | | |
|---|---|---|
| | | |

I can put the body parts puzzle together.

Not Mastered/In Progress/Mastered

| | | |
|---|---|---|
| | | |

I can find the left side of my drawing paper.

Not Mastered/In Progress/Mastered

| | | |
|---|---|---|
| | | |

I can find the right side of my drawing paper.

Name _____

Date _____

Progress Chart

## POSITION-IN-SPACE PERCEPTION
### (continued)

Not Mastered/In Progress/Mastered

| | | |
|---|---|---|
| | | |

I can distinguish my left side from my right side. (Laterality)

Not Mastered/In Progress/Mastered

| | | |
|---|---|---|
| | | |

I can move, on command, to the left, right, in front, or in back of another object.

Not Mastered/In Progress/Mastered

| | | |
|---|---|---|
| | | |

I can place objects, on command, to the left, right, in front, or in back of each other.

## PERCEIVING SPATIAL RELATIONSHIPS

Spatial relationship perception is closely related to position-in-space perception. Therefore, it will be the next perceptual area discussed. Some of the same activities develop both areas.

## THE IMPORTANCE OF THE SKILL

Perception of spatial relationships is the ability to relate the position of two or more objects to oneself and to each other.

Don't confuse this with position-in-space perception (the relationship of the child's body to his or her environment). Spatial relationships consist of the position of two other objects in relation to each other and to the child's body (different but interrelated).

Spatial relationship perception is a later skill, one that is more complicated and demanding in the interpretative process. A certain amount of visual memory must be involved. The child must be able to remember sequences of objects and placement in relation to each other away from himself.

Simple patterns can be remembered in verbal form. A person stringing beads can say to himself, "2 red, 2 white, 2 red," and so on. But a weaver copying a complicated pattern must constantly retain a mental picture of the whole pattern while he or she attends to details of line directions, distances of color and shapes, changes in pattern, and connection of angles.

Visual memory of a word and its parts requires as intricate a mind process as that of the weaver's pattern. Thus, the skill or lack of it bears on spelling and reading.

Difficulty in interpreting spatial relationships leads to confusion in learning to interpret a symbolic language. The child may read the word "sprung" as "spurring" but spell it as "s-u-p-n-r-g."

Many other tasks such as model making, graph reading, and the interpretation of measurements may also prove to be difficult if spatial relationship perception is deficient.

Learning to write will be a difficult task. If children cannot work with lines and spaces in relation to themselves, they will be unable to form letters correctly. The letters may be written in reverse, upside down, or floating in space, or they may be incorrectly proportioned to one another.

Just a few minutes a day can help prevent or overcome this problem. Below are some easy, enjoyable activities that can be used. These activities can be practiced by small groups or by individuals working with classmates who have mastered specific skills. The materials described are made of common everyday items usually found around the house or in the classroom. You can request that the children bring some of these items from home.

## MATERIALS TO GATHER

One roll of brown paper

Felt-tipped markers, wide and fine point

Yarn or string

Glue or paste

Construction paper, assorted colors

Full-length mirror

Beads or spools

## ACTIVITIES THAT BUILD SPATIAL RELATIONSHIP PERCEPTION

The following activities will help develop your students' spatial relationship perception. Be sure the concept is understood by each student.

Materials:        Posterboard or cardboard
                  Scissors
                  Pencil
                  Fine line felt-tipped pens

Construction:     On a piece of posterboard or cardboard, draw a large
                  freehand design in pencil. Cut out the separate shapes
                  that were formed. Use these shapes to trace many other
                  designs on larger pieces of board. Outline these designs
                  in fine line felt-tipped pen. The traced designs will not be
                  cut out but will be used as patterns.

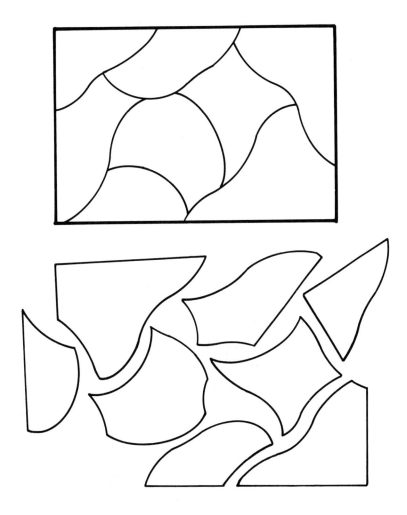

Activity:         The child will use the separate design patterns to fit each
                  shape onto the large patterns. After he or she completes
                  the patterns, an attempt may be made to form the same
                  design beside the completed one.

**55**

Materials:           One piece of plywood, 10″×10″
                     Nails and hammer
                     Yarn
                     Rubber bands, 3 colors
                     Ruler
                     Magic marker, black

Construction:        On the piece of plywood, measure and draw lines two
                     inches apart, both vertically and horizontally. At each
                     point where the lines cross, partially hammer in a nail.

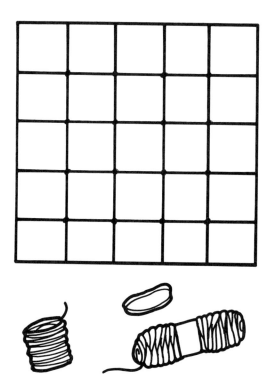

Activity:            Using yarn, string or rubber bands, the child forms
                     designs around the nails. Only straight-edged shapes will
                     be accomplished. Discuss this fact with the child and
                     have him or her experiment and verbalize.

Materials:          Posterboard, 3 colors
                    Tagboard patterns of basic shapes
                    Pencil and fine line felt-tipped pens
                    Scissors

Construction:       Cut triangles, rectangles, and squares in several colors
                    using the tagboard patterns for tracing. On larger pieces
                    of posterboard, trace a pattern and shape it in the same
                    colors as the shapes you have cut. Start with simple designs
                    of a few pieces and expand to more complicated designs.

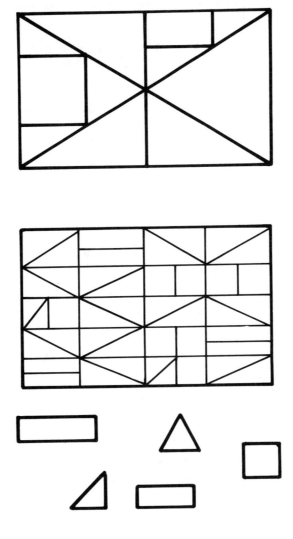

Activity:           Starting with the simple design boards, the child is to lay
                    the colored shapes directly on the corresponding shapes
                    in the design pattern. After simpler ones are mastered,
                    more complicated patterns may be used.

**57**

3-9. String Along

Materials:        Colored beads or painted spools
Posterboard, white
$3'' \times 5''$ index cards, unlined
Shoestrings or heavy twine
Marking pens

Construction:    If you do not have colored beads, collect and paint old
thread spools. Draw and color sequence patterns on
$3'' \times 5''$ cards or posterboard.

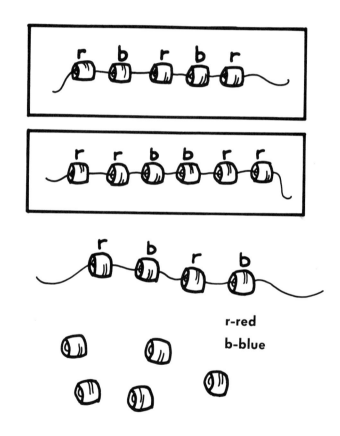

r–red

b–blue

Activity:          The child uses the $3'' \times 5''$ pattern cards as models. He or
she threads the shoestring or twine through the beads or
spools, copying the order of color shown on the card.

Materials:              One box of flat toothpicks
                        Black construction paper
                        Glue

Construction:           On black construction paper, $10'' \times 12''$, paste toothpicks in
                        free designs. Start with simple designs and few lines and
                        then graduate to more complex formations.

Activity:               The pupil is supplied with black paper, toothpicks, and
                        the model designs to copy. The simplest design is copied
                        first. Then, the pupil gradually works through the more
                        complex formations.

Name _____

Date _____

## Progress Chart

### SPATIAL RELATIONSHIP PERCEPTION

Not Mastered/In Progress/Mastered

| | | |
|---|---|---|
| | | |

I can compare animals or objects to myself using terms such as: bigger, smaller, taller, shorter, or thinner.

Not Mastered/In Progress/Mastered

| | | |
|---|---|---|
| | | |

I can draw facial features in correct position.

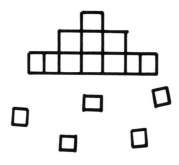

Not Mastered/In Progress/Mastered

| | | |
|---|---|---|
| | | |

I can use blocks to copy a block design.

Name _____

Date _____

## Progress Chart

## SPATIAL RELATIONSHIP PERCEPTION
(continued)

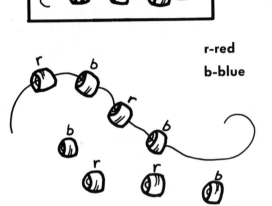

**r-red**

**b-blue**

I can match a pattern when stringing beads.

Not Mastered/In Progress/Mastered

| | | |
|---|---|---|
| | | |

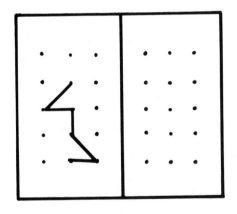

I can draw an exact copy of a dot-to-dot pattern.

Not Mastered/In Progress/Mastered

| | | |
|---|---|---|
| | | |

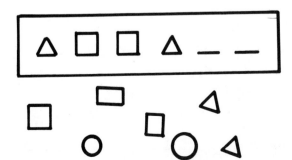

I can correctly complete an unfinished pattern sequence.

Not Mastered/In Progress/Mastered

| | | |
|---|---|---|
| | | |

# FIGURE-GROUND DIFFERENTIATION

Figure-ground differentiation is the ability to keep attention on the main object among other objects. The main object is the figure to which the attention is drawn. All other objects become the background but are still in view of the individual. For example, in a picture of a house, trees, clouds, flowers, and birds, the house would be the main point of attention. The other objects merely fill space in the background and do not draw attention toward them. Although they are seen and recognized, attention remains on the house figure.

Another example of the figure being the center of attention is this: A little girl puts down a ball (which was her center figure of attention), then picks up a pail. The pail becomes the center figure in her field of vision and the ball becomes part of the background.

# THE IMPORTANCE OF THE SKILL

A child with poor figure-ground ability appears to be very inattentive and disorganized because his or her attention jumps to any other object that intrudes on the visual field. He or she has great difficulty concentrating on one item or task. This child's attention span (length of time that he or she can concentrate on one task) will be short and sporadic.

Such a child may have difficulty drawing a straight line between boundaries because the boundaries catch their attention. Therefore letters are formed incorrectly and not in proper relationship to one another on the page.

Also, the difficulty of transferring focus of attention results in scanning problems. This child appears careless in his or her work because of an inability to keep the place on a page or to locate specific words in a sentence or in the dictionary.

At home, the child is unable to find a specific object even when it is out in the open.

In school, figure-ground weaknesses make it impossible for the student to analyze a word because he or she may fuse the letters together. This would create a different visual image in the decoding process. For example: The word "clip" may become "dip" as the child would fuse the "c" to the "l", thus reading it as the letter "d".

Training in figure-ground discrimination should result in improved ability to follow a line of print, maintain attention to the work at hand while ignoring surrounding background, and in general better organized behavior patterns.

# MATERIALS TO GATHER

Small paper bags

Construction paper, assorted

Manila paper, 12″ × 18″

Posterboard, assorted

Assorted nails

Small, half-pint milk cartons, six to nine

Staples

Alphabet cereal or macaroni

Egg cartons

Burlap

Assorted objects from home or school

Pencils

Hanging shoe bag with pockets

One small bucket or trash can

Scissors

Glue

Scraps of cloth or wallpaper

Cellophane tape

Old story books containing pictures

Felt

Alphabet templates, 3″

Envelopes

Felt-tipped pens, assorted colors

Self-closing storage bags

Clear self-stick vinyl

Crayons, plastic

## ACTIVITIES THAT BUILD FIGURE-GROUND DIFFERENTIATION

The following activities will help develop your students' figure-ground differentiation. Be sure the concept is understood by each student.

Materials:          Posterboard
                    4 to 6 small paper bags
                    Construction paper
                    Catalogues
                    Scissors
                    Glue

Construction:       Cut out pictures of objects that contain shapes within
                    their structure. Glue these onto construction paper. On
                    the small bags draw the shapes that are to be recognized
                    within the objects. Glue those bags to a posterboard.

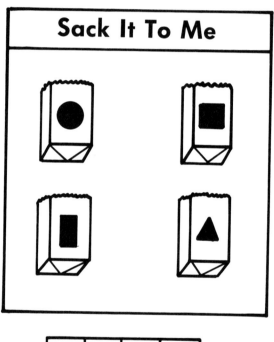

Activity:           The pupils remove all pictures and sort them into correct
                    sacks based on the particular shape shown within them.
                    For example: A coffee table picture will be placed in the
                    bag containing a rectangle because of the table top shape.

**Materials:**
Magazines
Old story books
Construction paper
Scissors
Glue
Clear self-stick vinyl

**Construction:** Cut out large pictures of heads, bodies, and different objects. Glue each one to large pieces of construction paper. Cover with clear self-stick vinyl. Cut each picture as shown and store in envelopes.

b. Cut objects vertically.

a. Cut faces horizontally.

c. Cut animals along neck, shoulders, waist and tail.

**Activity:** Pupils remove pieces and assemble each puzzle. Notice that in (a) and (b) all of the pieces are the same shape.

3-13. Block-O

Materials:          Posterboard
Broad-tipped marking pens
Box of colored counting blocks
Large self-closing storage bag

Construction:     Cut strips of posterboard, 5″ × 7″. On each strip make
design patterns using colored squares. Place five design
strips and enough blocks to complete each design in a
storage bag.

r-red
b-blue
g-green
y-yellow
o-orange

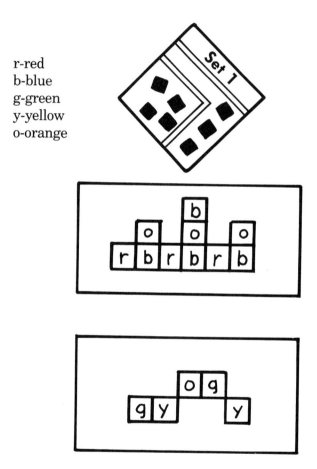

Activity:          Pupils take a storage bag set, remove the cards, and
assemble the blocks on the colored designs. Later, they
assemble the same design off the card.

Materials:          Tagboard shape templates
                    Manila paper
                    Pencils
                    Crayons

Construction:       None. The construction is in the activity.

 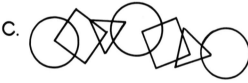

Activity:           a. Using one shape, overlap and outline with pencil.
                       Then, trace over each shape with a different color and
                       shade the inside.
                    b. Use two shapes in overlapping.
                    c. Use three or more shapes in overlapping.

Materials:          Posterboard
                    Marking pens
                    Clear self-stick vinyl
                    Plastic crayons

Construction:       Cut posterboard strips, 5″ × 7″. On each strip write two
                    words, superimposed over one another. Write the answers
                    on back.

Activity:           Pupils use plastic crayons to trace the words on each
                    card. Each word should be traced in a different color. The
                    back may be referred to for self-checking.

Name _____

Date _____

Progress Chart

## FIGURE-GROUND DIFFERENTIATION

Not Mastered/In Progress/Mastered

| | | |
|---|---|---|
| | | |

I can keep attention on a task until it is completed.

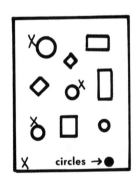

Not Mastered/In Progress/Mastered

| | | |
|---|---|---|
| | | |

I can find specific shapes hidden among many objects or shapes.

Not Mastered/In Progress/Mastered

| | | |
|---|---|---|
| | | |

I can complete puzzles.

Name ————————————————

Date ————————————————

**Progress Chart**

## FIGURE-GROUND DIFFERENTIATION
### (continued)

Not Mastered/In Progress/Mastered

| | | |
|---|---|---|
| | | |

I can locate specific words or letters in a story.

Not Mastered/In Progress/Mastered

| | | |
|---|---|---|
| | | |

I can read without losing my place on the page.

## CONSTANCY PERCEPTION

Constancy perception is the ability to recognize that an object is the same or has the same characteristics, such as shape, position, or size, regardless of the angle or the way it is presented.

For example: A rectangle is always a rectangle regardless of how it is shown.

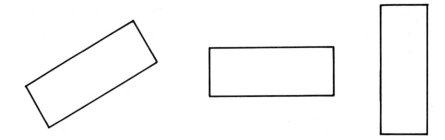

Also, each letter is the same regardless of its placement within different words. For example, an "a" is an "a" in chalk, apple, Agnes, and the like.

## THE IMPORTANCE OF THE SKILL

Exercises that stress perceptual constancy help a child discriminate size, shape, and color and recognize three dimensional objects. After this development is accomplished, the child will be able to transfer to the discrimination of two dimensional copies of the objects, and then to print.

If a child has difficulty in constancy perception, he or she may not recognize words that are the same but in different contexts. Perhaps the child can read the word cards one-at-a-time, but cannot recognize these same known words in a sentence or story.

Also, such a child will find it difficult to distinguish small details within letters and words such as:

| "r" | from an | "n" | r – r |
| "h" | from an | "n" | h – n |
| "a" | from a | "d" | a – d |
| "w" | from a | "v" | w – v |
| "u" | from an | "n" | u – n |

The process of transfer to print and paper is often not an automatic one. It is frequently dependent on specific training. This training should start with three-dimensional objects, such as the ones suggested here, and then progress to two-dimensional (print on paper) objects, letters, and words.

1. Have the child sort objects according to the same shape, same color, and same size. Later add texture to the choices.

2. Expose two objects. Have the child pick out the largest or smallest one.

3. Add two pairs of objects with less noticeable size differences. The child is to pick up the largest or smallest of the objects.

4. Add a third size and have the child select the items that are small, medium, and large, in that order.

5. Show the child a basic shape (square, circle, rectangle, or triangle). Have the child find something in the room that has the same shape. For example if a rectangle is shown, the child may locate a door, window, book, or table.

6. Coloring books are useful for transfer to two-dimensional representation. Have the child look for and outline in crayon any object in the pictures that have the shapes of a circle, rectangle, square, or triangle.

7. Let the child paste toothpicks on dark colored construction paper, forming basic shapes that contain straight edges or just making designs.

8. Let the child twist and form shapes or make free form designs using pipe cleaners and patterns.

9. Supply yarn for the child to use in laying out shapes. With yarn, children can also make curved shapes.

10. When the child is learning the alphabet, let him or her form the letter shapes with yarn or clay, using pattern cards as guides.

11. To aid in recognition of specific letters or words, let the child search to find specific letters or words in the newspapers or magazines and circle these with a bright colored crayon or felt-tipped pen.

## MATERIALS TO GATHER

Assorted objects or various sizes, colors, and textures

Basic shape templates

Black construction paper

Assorted colors of construction paper

Toothpicks

Pipe-cleaners

Yarn

Clay

Manila paper, 12″ × 18″

Old catalogues

Magazines

Scissors

Glue

Felt-tipped pens

Cookie sheet

Index cards, unlined

Salt or sand

Shoe boxes

Clothespins

Chalkboard

Chalk

Razor blade, single-edged

Yellow tempera paint

Brush, ½″

Clear self-stick vinyl

File folders

## ACTIVITIES THAT BUILD CONSTANCY PERCEPTION

The following activities will help develop your students' constancy perception by moving from three-dimensional objects to two-dimensional activities. Be sure the concept is understood by each student.

Materials:          Catalogues
                    Construction paper
                    Scissors
                    Glue

Construction:       Cut and paste four pictures of each object on cards
                    3″ × 3″. Each picture should show the objects in a
                    different position or at a different angle. Find four objects
                    for each game.

Activity:           Pupils match cards that contain pictures that are of the
                    same thing, regardless of the position or angle.

Materials:        Chalkboard
                  Cardboard
                  Chalk
                  Razor blade

Construction:     Using a razor blade, cut out cardboard basic shape
                  templates. These should be in various sizes. Save the
                  cardboard cutouts as well as the pieces of cardboard from
                  which they were cut.

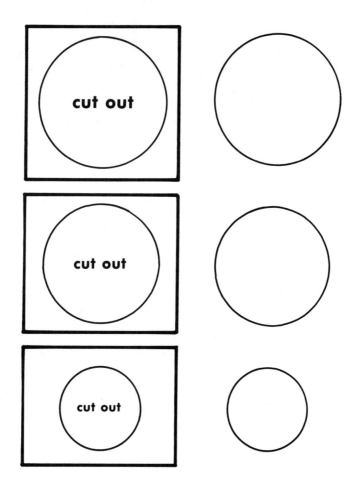

Activity:         Pupils trace the inner templates with their fingers, then
                  on chalkboards with chalk. Later, the shape pattern is
                  traced around the outside. This is to be continued until
                  the pupil has visual-kinesthetic memory of each shape.

Materials:              Black construction paper, $12'' \times 18''$
                        Yellow tempera paint
                        Brush
                        Clay
                        Clear self-stick vinyl

Construction:           On black construction paper, draw shapes turned in
                        different directions and in varying sizes with yellow
                        tempera paint. Place one shape on each page. Cover with
                        clear self-stick vinyl.

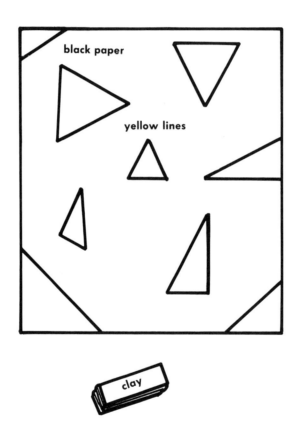

Activity:               Pupils use clay to roll and shape on each shape pattern.

76

Materials:         One cookie sheet or tray
                   Salt or sand
                   Unlined 3″×5″ cards

Construction:      Sprinkle salt or sand onto a cookie sheet. Write the words
                   being studied on cards for use as visual models.

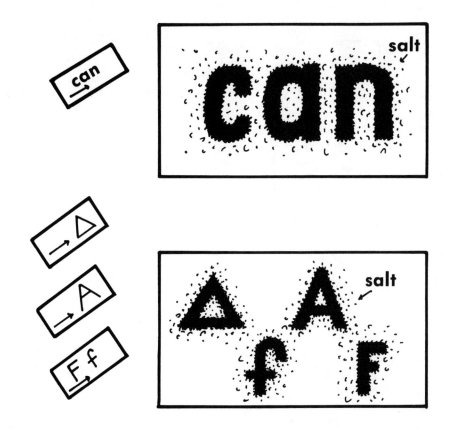

Activity:          Pupils trace shapes, letters, or words in the salt; then
                   shake the salt tray and trace again. This is done until
                   the model can be copied correctly from memory.

Name _____

Date _____

**Progress Chart**

## CONSTANCY PERCEPTION

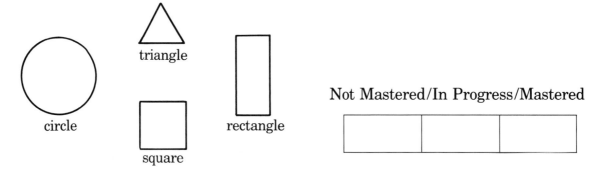

circle   triangle   square   rectangle

Not Mastered/In Progress/Mastered

| | | |
|---|---|---|
| | | |

I can recognize and name specific shapes.

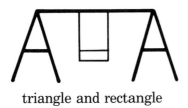

triangle and rectangle

Not Mastered/In Progress/Mastered

| | | |
|---|---|---|
| | | |

I recognize shapes in everyday objects.

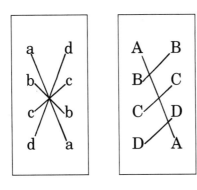

Not Mastered/In Progress/Mastered

| | | |
|---|---|---|
| | | |

I can match letters that are the same.

Name _____

Date _____

## Progress Chart

### CONSTANCY PERCEPTION
(continued)

| bear | dear | bean | bear |
|------|------|------|------|
| rag | rag | rug | bag |
| far | jar | far | car |

(bear), (bear), (rag), (rag), (far), (far) circled

Not Mastered/In Progress/Mastered

|  |  |  |
|--|--|--|
|  |  |  |

I recognize words that are alike.

*the*

    *The* bear went for a walk. *The* little dog followed. Soon *the* turtle came along.

"Find the word *the* in the story.

Not Mastered/In Progress/Mastered

|  |  |  |
|--|--|--|
|  |  |  |

I can recognize and find specific letters or words in print.

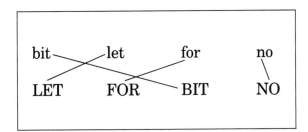

Not Mastered/In Progress/Mastered

|  |  |  |
|--|--|--|
|  |  |  |

I recognize words as being the same in different print.

## VISUAL-MOTOR DEVELOPMENT

Visual-motor development is the ability to coordinate vision with movements of the body. Smooth accomplishments of every action depend on adequate eye-hand coordination.

## THE IMPORTANCE OF THE SKILL

The sensory motor functions that develop during the first twelve to eighteen months are necessary for the child's ability to discriminate sights and sounds, and his ability to focus attention. During this phase, the child learns to grasp spatial location (place), time sequences (when steps occur), and sequential order through movement. This learning is important because the development of oral, written, and printed language is sequential. Speech is uttered in correct sequence of form. Writing must have correct syntax form in order to express ideas clearly. And words in print must contain the correct sequence of letters.

Between seven and eight years of age, visual perceptual development tapers off. All the visual perceptual abilities needed for successful school learning are within the experience of the average six- to eight-year-old.

Some aspects of the school curriculum concerned with the improvement of sensory-motor development are: physical education, arts and crafts using three-dimensional objects to train visual motor and fine motor coordination, and exercises to improve eye-hand coordination and eye tracking.

Movement education can improve a child's self-control. It requires concentration and self-monitoring, and body control leads to self-mastery.

Every child needs at least thirty minutes of supervised play and movement education daily. Children with any learning problems need intensive movement education because they are characteristically deficient in movement skills.

Weaknesses in eye-hand motor coordination can hamper the child's ability to master writing skills. Much of reading instruction and reinforcement is accomplished through writing skills.

Also, jerky eye movements create a slow and laborious approach to reading. This frustration, of course, would turn a child against reading as an enjoyable experience.

Training should begin with gross-motor, large muscle development, and progress to fine-motor development of smaller muscles. The large muscles must be trained before the small muscles can be brought under control. Finer development is necessary for smooth eye movement across a line of print and smooth eye-hand coordination in writing. The following training activities are suggested.

### Gross-Motor (large muscle) Development

1. *ANGELS IN THE SNOW:* The child lies on his or her back on the floor with legs together and arms to the sides. Both arms are moved along the floor (keeping floor contact) until they are above the head. At the count of

two, the arms are returned to the sides. The leg movements are done separately at first. At the count of one, the child slides her legs apart along the floor. At the count of two, the legs are brought back together. When the child can do arm and leg movements smoothly, they can be combined. At the count of one, the arms move out and up and the legs move apart simultaneously. At the count of two, arms and legs return to their original positions. Sometimes the words "open" and "close" make it easier for the child to follow the oral directions.

2.  *TRUNK LIFT:* The child lies face down a with his stomach on a pillow, and his hands clasped behind his head and neck. The child then raises his trunk off the floor. If the child cannot accomplish this, hold his feet down until his back muscles are strengthened.

3.  Creeping and crawling activities help to establish movement patterns that are bilateral.

    a.  Unilateral crawl (first): The child gets on his hands and knees and moves by lifting his right arm and right leg together. When this movement is developed, go into a bilateral crawl (right arm, left leg moving together; left arm, right leg moving together).

    b.  Creeping obstacle course: The room is set up so that the child must go under a table, around chairs, over boxes, along strings or narrow tape, between markers, on blocks, up and down steps, forward sideways, and backward.

    c.  Walking obstacle course: The child accomplishes this standing up rather than on her hands and knees. A ladder is placed flat on the floor or masking tape is laid in the shape of a ladder. The child walks, alternating feet between the rungs, swinging opposite arms forward with each step, turning the head to the side on which the leg is advancing.

4.  Balance Board Activities:

    a.  A balance board ($2'' \times 4'' \times 6''$) is laid on the floor. The child stands on this and tries to balance. While balancing, he or she can try to catch a ball, recite a poem, repeat number combinations, and so on.

    b.  The child balances a ruler on her head, then a yard stick, and finally a book while walking forward heel to toe. Next, walk toe to heel backward; then, sideways to the left and right. Have an eye level target for the child to focus on while moving across the board.

5.  More Coordination Activities:

    a.  Have the pupils stand for ten seconds on tiptoe (both legs, then one at a time). Stand on one foot and sling the other leg out to the front, side, and rear.

    b.  With eyes opened and closed, have the children skip, gallop, and hop on one foot and both feet. Then, ask them to perform standing high jumps, emphasizing use of the arms for balance.

c. Play imaginative games (using pulling, pushing, and running movements) by pretending that the children are the wind, rain, thunder, and lightning.

## Fine Motor Development

6. Have the children put puzzles together to form a picture.

7. Finger painting is good practice for control. Make cheap paint using liquid starch and food coloring if cost is a concern.

8. Direct pupils to fold papers according to oral directions.

9. Drawing lines connecting dots is excellent practice.

10. String beads following a specific sequential pattern.

11. Let the children copy a design that you have drawn on the board using simple-lined shapes.

12. Have the pupils trace geometric forms with one finger; then, with pencils.

13. Have the children trace large letters with a pencil or in a salt-filled cooky sheet.

14. Supply broad crayons and newspapers to practice making full arm swing circles, sticks, and curves (a prewriting activity).

15. Draw a different maze on the board each week. Let a child follow the maze with a finger, then chalk.

## One-Minute Eye Movement Exercises to Train Left to Right Progression Without Losing Focus

16. Hold an object stationary in front of a child. He or she should try to focus on the object while moving the head from left to right. Then, while moving the head up and down, in a nodding motion and with a rolling motion, the child should try to retain focus. This exercise should be done slowly, each day, until it can be successfully accomplished.

17. Help the child follow a rolling ball as far as possible without moving his head. This will aid in developing smooth eye movement.

18. Hang a ball from the ceiling. Have the child follow the ball movements without moving her head. Swing the ball from side to side, then away from and toward the child.

19. Tie a ribbon to a Hula Hoop and then turn the hoop in various directions in front of the child. The child is to retain focus on the ribbon at all times.

## MATERIALS TO GATHER

| | |
|---|---|
| Masking tape | Newsprint, unlined and 1″ lined |
| Balls, assorted sizes | Buttons |
| Rope | Shoe laces |

Hula Hoop

Ruler

Rags

Empty coffee cans,
   3 lb. size or larger

Strong nylon cord, ½″ thick

Chalkboards

Chalk

Newspaper

Red crayons

Finger paints

Fingerpaint paper

Snaps, very large

Zippers

Velcro strips, 1″

Scissors, blunt end and some left-handed

Felt-tipped pens

Hole puncher, single

Paddle and ball

Heavy twine

Posterboard, black

Yellow paint

Paint brush, 1″

## ACTIVITIES THAT BUILD VISUAL-MOTOR DEVELOPMENT

The following activities will help develop your students' visual-motor skills. Be sure the concept is understood by each student.

| | |
|---|---|
| Materials: | Jumping ropes, 6<br>Records<br>Record player<br>Six balls, 6″–8″ diameter |
| Construction: | Place taped squares and a taped ladder on the classroom floor. The activities are carried out while music is being played. |

| | |
|---|---|
| Activity: | Six pupils are to bounce the balls within taped squares while balancing on one foot at a time (a). Six pupils are to jump rope between the ladder rungs using both feet, then one foot at a time (b). |

Materials: Chalkboards
Chalk, 2 pieces per child
Newspapers
Masking tape
Large red crayons

Construction: If chalkboards are available, there is no construction. If not, tape newspaper high on a wall or door and use red crayon.

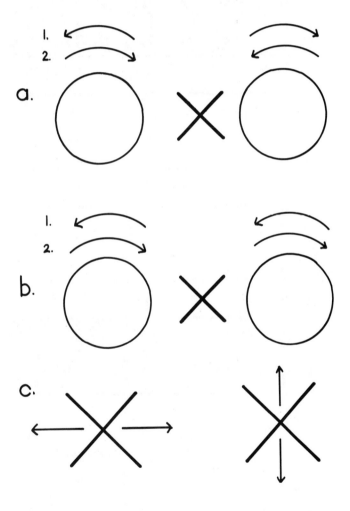

Activity: Have the pupils place an "X" at eye level. Throughout movements in a, b, and c, above, the eyes are to remain focused on the X. The pupils use chalk on the chalkboards or red crayon on the newspaper.

85

Materials:        Scissors
                  Marking pens
                  Newspapers

Construction:     Draw curved lines and zigzag lines on newspaper strips.

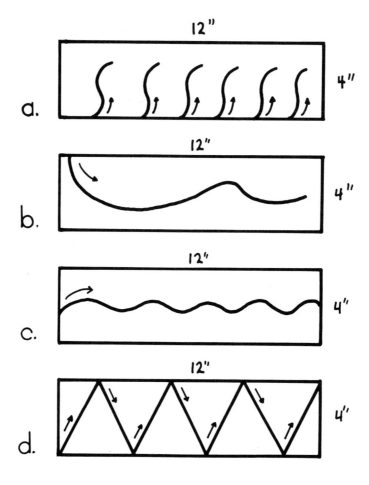

Activity:         Pupils cut paper following bold lines and arrow
                  directions.

Materials:            Newsprint, unlined, 12″ × 18″
                      Marking pens
                      Red crayon
                      Masking tape

Construction:         On newsprint, draw bold curves and lines, then draw
                      dotted curves and lines. See samples below.

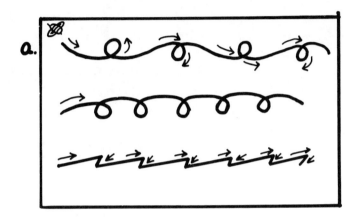

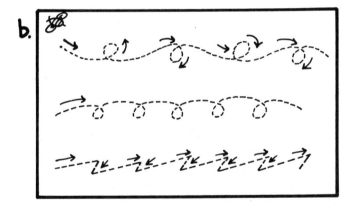

Activity:             Pupils are to trace over the bold lined bee trail with red
                      crayon. When this has been mastered, the pupil traces
                      over a dotted trail with red crayon.

Materials:          Newsprint, unlined
                    Felt-tipped pens
                    Hole puncher

Construction:       With felt-tipped pens, draw curved lines on newsprint
                    strips that have been cut to $2'' \times 10''$.

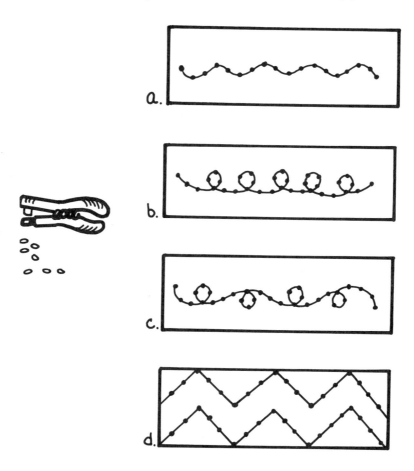

Activity:           Using a hole puncher, the pupil follows the bee trail.
                    Later, he or she can punch the same pattern on blank
                    strips, referring to the model strips as patterns.

Name —————————————————————

Date —————————————————————

## Progress Chart

## VISUAL-MOTOR DEVELOPMENT

I can hop on either foot.

Not Mastered/In Progress/Mastered

| | | |
|---|---|---|
| | | |

I can skip.

Not Mastered/In Progress/Mastered

| | | |
|---|---|---|
| | | |

I can jump with both feet off the ground.

Not Mastered/In Progress/Mastered

| | | |
|---|---|---|
| | | |

Name _____

Date _____

Progress Chart

## VISUAL-MOTOR DEVELOPMENT
### (continued)

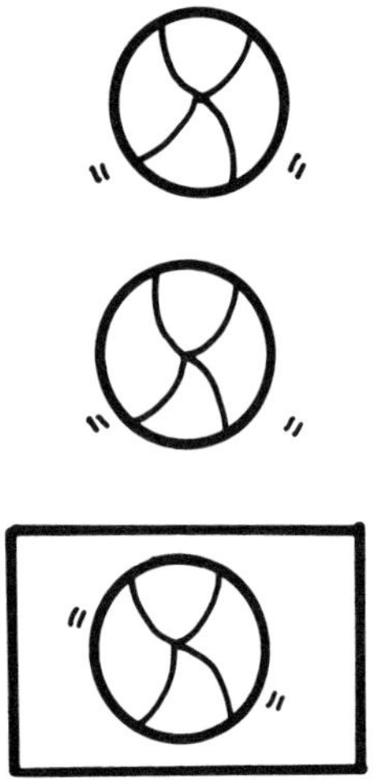

Not Mastered/In Progress/Mastered

| | | |
|---|---|---|
| | | |

I can bounce a ball within a taped square.

Not Mastered/In Progress/Mastered

| | | |
|---|---|---|
| | | |

I can balance while walking on a straight line or board.

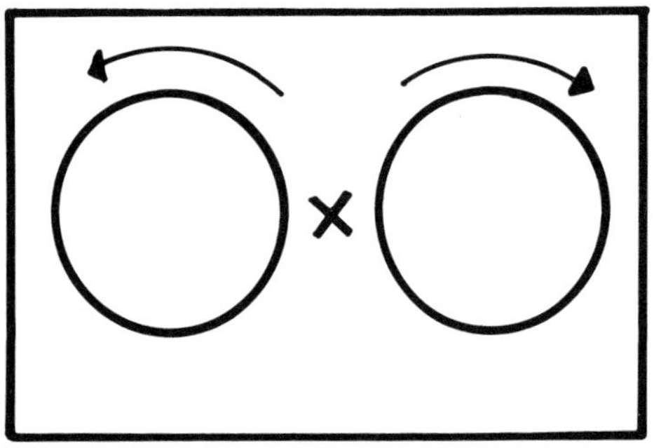

Not Mastered/In Progress/Mastered

| | | |
|---|---|---|
| | | |

I can make well-rounded circles using bilateral arm movements.

Name ———————————————————

Date ———————————————————

## Progress Chart

## VISUAL-MOTOR DEVELOPMENT
### (continued)

I can use scissors properly.

Not Mastered/In Progress/Mastered

| | | |
|---|---|---|
| | | |

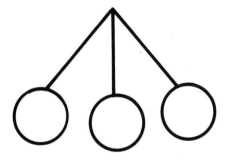

I can follow a moving target without moving my head.

Not Mastered/In Progress/Mastered

| | | |
|---|---|---|
| | | |

I can catch and throw a ball.

Not Mastered/In Progress/Mastered

| | | |
|---|---|---|
| | | |

Name _____

Date _____

## VISUAL PERCEPTION SKILLS CHECKLIST

### POSITION-IN-SPACE PERCEPTION

1. Completes body puzzles. _____
2. Distinguishes left and right sides of a page. _____
3. Distinguishes left and right sides of the body. _____
4. Moves on command to the left, right, front, or back of an object. _____
5. Manipulates objects to the left, right, front, or back of each other. _____

### SPATIAL RELATIONSHIPS PERCEPTION

1. Makes comparisons using size concepts. _____
2. Places facial features in correct position. _____
3. Copies a block design using blocks and patterns. _____
4. Duplicates a bead pattern. _____
5. Correctly executes dot-to-dot patterns. _____
6. Correctly finishes an unfinished pattern sequence. _____

### FIGURE-GROUND DIFFERENTIATION

1. Keeps attention on a task until it is complete. _____
2. Locates specific shapes among many shapes. _____
3. Completes puzzles. _____
4. Locates specific words on a page. _____
5. Reads without losing place on a page. _____

Name _____

Date _____

VISUAL PERCEPTION SKILLS CHECKLIST
(continued)

## CONSTANCY PERCEPTION

1. Recognizes and names basic shapes. _____
2. Recognizes shapes in everyday objects. _____
3. Discriminates letters that are alike. _____
4. Discriminates words that are alike. _____
5. Locates specific letters or words in print. _____
6. Recognizes words as being the same in different styles of print. _____

## VISUAL-MOTOR DEVELOPMENT

1. Hops on either foot. _____
2. Skips. _____
3. Jumps with both feet off the ground. _____
4. Bounces a ball within a confined area. _____
5. Balances while walking on a straight line or board. _____
6. Executes well-rounded circles using bilateral arm movements. _____
7. Uses scissors correctly. _____
8. Follows a moving target without moving the head. _____
9. Catches and throws a ball. _____

Key: ✔ Skill mastered
X Needs further instruction

## CHAPTER FOUR

# Building Auditory Perception Skills

Auditory perception is another interpretive ability that can be achieved through training. To be able to discriminate between sounds is basic to obtaining word attack skills in reading.

The major subskills of auditory perception that affect reading will be discussed in this chapter. They are: auditory figure-ground differentiation, auditory discrimination, auditory memory and sequencing, and auditory sound-blending.

## AUDITORY FIGURE-GROUND DIFFERENTIATION

Auditory figure-ground differentiation is the ability to keep one's attention on specific sounds while ignoring other sounds in the background; but, it includes being able to change one's focus of attention. For example: While listening to a neighbor, you will also hear when a child calls. When on the phone, you will still hear the doorbell. A driver listens to the car radio but will also hear another car horn.

## THE IMPORTANCE OF THE SKILL

During reading instruction, much time is spent on listening for and recognizing sounds. If a child is completely distracted by any additional sound that may occur, he or she will not be able to attend to the lesson being presented. Thus, the child must be trained to ignore any noise not relevant to the instruction.

As with all learning skills, the training activities for this area are begun in the home. However, when you are talking with your pupils or giving oral directions to be followed, these skills can be sharpened as the children learn to listen and to attend to specific directions.

## AUDITORY DISCRIMINATION

Auditory discrimination is the ability to distinguish one sound from another. It is a comparison of sounds, rather than attention to only one specific sound while background noises are occurring, as in figure-ground differentiation.

## THE IMPORTANCE OF THE SKILL

It is necessary for pupils to be able to distinguish between common sounds (gross discrimination) before they can be expected to recognize sounds that are closely related (fine discrimination).

A child who cannot distinguish similarities and differences between sounds will be unable to use the phonetic approach to reading. The child's ability to spell may also be hampered.

## MATERIALS TO GATHER

Record player                                    Rice
Records of farm animal sounds                    Dried beans
Blank tapes                                      Salt or sand
Catalogues and magazines                         Macaroni
Construction paper                               Large grocery bags
Scissors                                         Crayons
Glue                                             Whistle
Pictures of farm animals                         Kitchen timer
Paper bags                                       Blindfold
Recorded stories                                 Tambourine
Drum                                             Triangle
Glass                                            Bells
Bell                                             Xylophone
Book                                             Flutophone
Balloons                                         Musical Tone Blocks
Baby food jars, 8                                Plastic tape, red, yellow, and blue

## ACTIVITIES THAT BUILD AUDITORY FIGURE-GROUND DIFFERENTIATION AND AUDITORY DISCRIMINATION

The following activities will help develop your students' auditory figure-ground differentiation and discrimination. Be sure the concepts are understood by each student.

4-1. When Did I Speak?  *Auditory Discrimination*

Materials:  Farm animal tapes or records
Tape recorder or record player
Pictures of farm animals, 2 each
Posterboard
Construction paper
Scissors
Glue

Construction:  Paste pictures of animals on a piece of construction paper, 3″ × 3″. Make pockets of construction paper by gluing the bottom and ends of a strip of folded paper the length of a posterboard. Divide each row in thirds by marking with dark pen and number each pocket. Make two sets. On the back of each picture place the numeral which corresponds to the ordinal position of each sound on tape. Attach an envelope to the back for storage of small pictures.

1. horse    2. mule    3. pig    4. rooster
5. chick    6. turkey    7. sheep    8. cow
9. dog

Activity:  Play a tape. As each animal speaks the children turn off the tape and place the appropriate picture in the correct numbered pocket. When completed, the pictures are in correct order of their sounds.

Materials:        Story recording of Little Red Riding Hood
                  Record player
                  Paper bags
                  Construction paper
                  Scissors
                  Glue

Construction:     Make bag puppets of Little Red Riding Hood, the mother,
                  the wolf, and grandmother.

Activity:         Play the recorded story. As each voice is identified, the
                  pupil who has the correct bag puppet stands and holds
                  up the bag.

Materials:            Recorded story of The Three Bears
                      Record player
                      Large grocery bags
                      Crayons
                      Construction paper
                      Scissors
                      Glue

Construction:         Make large characters of Goldilocks and the Three Bears
                      to fit over the child's head and shoulders.

Activity:             As the recorded story is being played, the character
                      speaking steps forward and demonstrates actions in the
                      plot.

Materials:    Drum
              Tambourine
              Triangle
              Bells
              Xylophone
              Flutophone

Construction:  None

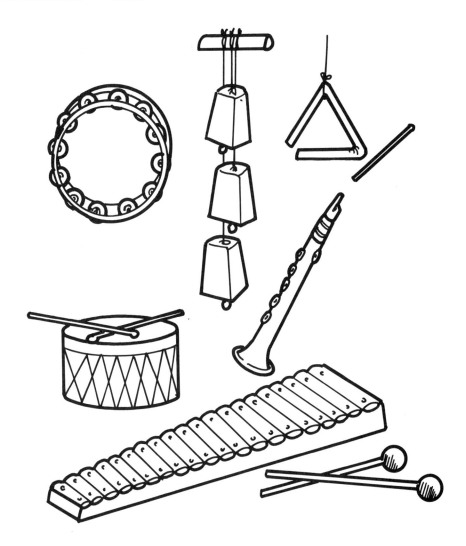

Activity:     While pupils are watching, play each instrument. Then, with their eyes closed, the pupils are to name the instrument being played.

Name _____

Date _____

## Progress Chart

### AUDITORY FIGURE-GROUND DIFFERENTIATION
### and AUDITORY DISCRIMINATION

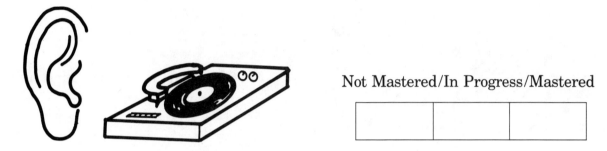

Not Mastered/In Progress/Mastered

| | | |
|---|---|---|
| | | |

I can listen and respond to a command while music is being played.

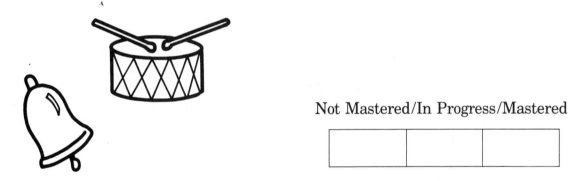

Not Mastered/In Progress/Mastered

| | | |
|---|---|---|
| | | |

I can recognize and name several sounds that are occurring at the same time.

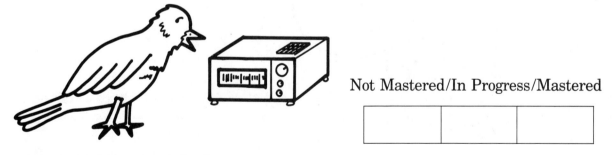

Not Mastered/In Progress/Mastered

| | | |
|---|---|---|
| | | |

I can recognize common sounds that are different.

Name _____

Date _____

## AUDITORY FIGURE-GROUND DIFFERENTIATION
### and AUDITORY DISCRIMINATION
#### (continued)

Not Mastered/In Progress/Mastered

| | | |
|---|---|---|
| | | |

I can recognize common sounds that are alike.

Not Mastered/In Progress/Mastered

| | | |
|---|---|---|
| | | |

I can recognize words that rhyme.

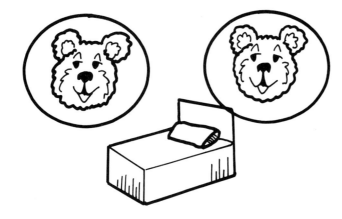

Not Mastered/In Progress/Mastered

| | | |
|---|---|---|
| | | |

I can recognize words that are the same.

Name _____

Date _____

## Progress Chart

### AUDITORY FIGURE-GROUND DIFFERENTIATION
### and AUDITORY DISCRIMINATION
### (continued)

Not Mastered/In Progress/Mastered

|  |  |  |
|---|---|---|
|  |  |  |

I can recognize words that are different.

Not Mastered/In Progress/Mastered

|  |  |  |
|---|---|---|
|  |  |  |

I can recognize words that start alike.

Not Mastered/In Progress/Mastered

|  |  |  |
|---|---|---|
|  |  |  |

I can recognize words that start with a different sound.

## AUDITORY MEMORY

Auditory memory is the skill of mentally storing information and remembering what one has heard.

## THE IMPORTANCE OF THE SKILL

This area is being developed when you are working on oral language usage and giving oral directions. It is tied in with auditory sequencing in reading. Not only what is heard but the order in which it is heard is very important.

## AUDITORY SEQUENCING

Auditory sequencing is the skill of remembering the order of items heard in a list; such as, the alphabet, months of the year, days of the week, and the like. Later the child can transfer to finer sequencing of speech sounds within words.

## THE IMPORTANCE OF THE SKILL

Reception of auditory stimuli always occurs in a specific sequence. Meaning is the result of keeping proper order. For example: r-e-a-d has a different meaning if the same letters are placed in a different sequence, such as, d-e-a-r.

A deficiency in auditory memory and sequencing will create problems in remembering the order of letters within words. It will also confuse the order of words within sentences and interfere with meaning.

## MATERIALS TO GATHER

Jars, 2

Pennies

Tissue paper

Construction paper, assorted colors

List of rhymes

Pictures that complete the rhymes

Scissors

Glue

Counting cubes, 18 red, 18 blue, 18 yellow

Beans, lima and pinto

File folders

Toy cars, 6

Envelopes

Tongue depressors

Wood stain or tempera paint

Juice cans, 16

White self-stick vinyl

Magazines

Coat hangers

Clothespins

Index cards, unlined
Felt-tipped pens
Self-closing plastic storage bags
Plastic play dishes
Posterboard
Box

Book of riddles
Tags
Paper clips
Cellophane tape
Hole puncher

Materials:     None

Construction:  None

Provide plenty of room for the children's movement and activity. Remove any obstacles that might create a hazard.

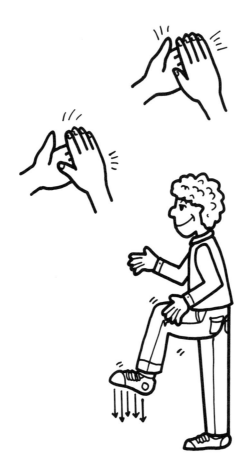

Activity:      You act out a short sequence of sounds for the children to imitate. Example: 2 claps, 1 stamp; 1 clap, 1 stamp, 1 clap. The children mimic your actions. Gradually increase the number of movements and sounds to be imitated.

Materials:          Pictures that complete the rhymes
                    Construction paper
                    List of rhymes being used
                    Scissors
                    Glue

Construction:       Glue pictures to construction paper or draw pictures to
                    display in front of the class.

I saw a *fox*
go into a _____ .

Kitty's in a *well.*
Ring a big _____ .

In a blue *boat*
I saw a white _____ .

We found a little *mouse*
inside the toy _____ .

In the blue *dish*
sat a gold _____ .

Activity:           Read rhymes to the pupils. Leave a key word out. The
                    pupils choose the picture that completes the rhyme and it
                    is read in complete form.

Materials:          File folders, 6
                    Toy cars, 6
                    Construction paper
                    Scissors
                    Glue

Construction:       Make 6 mystery road maps by gluing construction paper
                    squares as shown.

Activity:           Give 6 pupils a road map and toy car. Give oral travel
                    directions such as, "Move forward 3 moves, back up 1
                    move. Move ahead 6; then, go back 3 moves." If the moves
                    have been followed correctly, the pupils will reach the end
                    when you do.

Materials:          Tongue depressors
                    Wood stain or tempera paint
                    Juice cans, 16
                    Self-closing plastic storage bags
                    Self-stick vinyl
                    Index cards, unlined
                    Marking pens, assorted

Construction:       Cover juice cans with self-stick vinyl. Write ordinal words
                    on each can; such as, first, second, third, and fourth.
                    Paint tongue depressors. Make sequence color patterns
                    on index cards for checking.

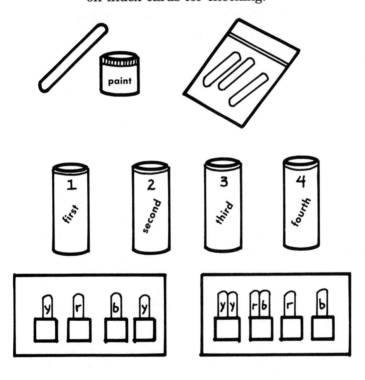

                    y-yellow     r-red      b-blue

Activity:           Give each child a set of tongue depressors and four
                    containers. A teacher or student orally directs the
                    sequence to be followed. The pupils place the same
                    colored tongue depressors in correct order, in the
                    containers. Expose the pattern cards for checking.

Materials:          Magazines and catalogues
Construction paper
Coat hangers
Clothespins
Scissors
Envelopes
Glue

Construction:     Choose three categories and cut out 3 to 4 pictures for each one. Paste these on a piece of construction paper 3″ × 3″. Write the titles on the envelope that will hold the pictures of all three categories. For example: Air, Sea, Land. Pictures will deal with planes, boats, cars, and the like. Attach clothespins and the envelope to a coat hanger.

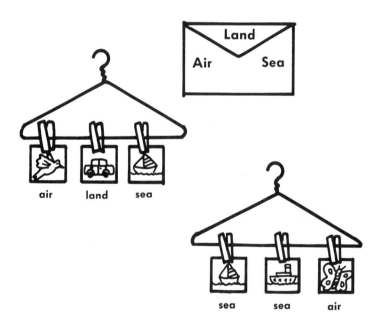

Activity:          Pupils spread pictures out on a table or desk so that each one is exposed. A student or teacher calls out the sequence of category by air, land, or sea; sea, sea, air, for example. Pupils choose pictures and clip them in order to the hangers. Any categories may be used to develop and expand this auditory sequencing game.

Name _____

Date _____

**Progress Chart**

## AUDITORY MEMORY and AUDITORY SEQUENCING

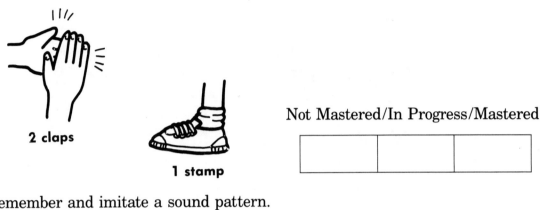

**2 claps**

**1 stamp**

Not Mastered/In Progress/Mastered

| | | |
|---|---|---|
| | | |

I can remember and imitate a sound pattern.

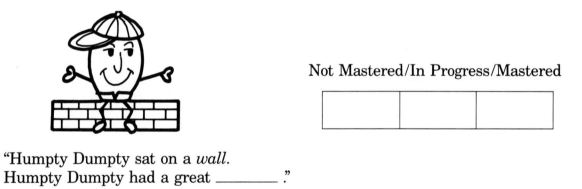

"Humpty Dumpty sat on a *wall*.
Humpty Dumpty had a great _____ ."

Not Mastered/In Progress/Mastered

| | | |
|---|---|---|
| | | |

I can remember and furnish missing rhyming words.

"Once upon a time...."

Not Mastered/In Progress/Mastered

| | | |
|---|---|---|
| | | |

I can listen to and retell a story.

Name _____

Date _____

**Progress Chart**

## AUDITORY MEMORY and AUDITORY SEQUENCING
### (continued)

I can say the alphabet in sequence.

Not Mastered/In Progress/Mastered

| | | |
|---|---|---|
| | | |

"Close the door; then, turn off the light."

I can listen to and follow oral directions.

Not Mastered/In Progress/Mastered

| | | |
|---|---|---|
| | | |

## AUDITORY SOUND-BLENDING

To recognize verbal sequences the child must understand how many sounds are heard in a word or how many words are heard in a sentence. This ability can be trained.

## THE IMPORTANCE OF THE SKILL

Sound-blending includes all of the auditory abilities. If a child is writing the word "cat," each sound and the sequence in which it occurs must be remembered. To simply remember that *cat* has three sounds which are *a, c,* and *t* is not sufficient. The word "cat" would possibly be spelled as a-t-c, t-a-c, or c-t-a if the child could not auditorily remember and blend the letters in correct sequence.

When children are learning to read, much time is spent in decoding (taking apart) each new word and analyzing each sound present. Then, these sounds must be strung together again, while blending each sound with the next, without distortion.

A child who cannot do this, is at a loss when a new word is met. No tool is available to be used independently. Each new word must be told and memorized as a sight word. This, of course, slows down progress in learning to read.

## MATERIALS TO GATHER

| | |
|---|---|
| Posterboard | Felt-tipped pens |
| Pictures of farm animals | Construction paper |
| Clear self-stick vinyl | Paper clips |
| Scissors | Index cards, unlined |
| Glue | Catalogues and magazines |

## ACTIVITIES THAT BUILD AUDITORY SOUND-BLENDING

The following activities will help develop your students' auditory sound-blending. Be sure the concept is understood by each student.

Materials: Posterboard
Farm animal pictures
Scissors
Glue
Clear self-stick vinyl

Construction: Cut posterboard into strips of 4″ × 18″. Glue farm animal pictures to the strips as shown. Start with two per strip then three per strip. Cover with clear self-stick vinyl.

(neigh)          (moo)

(nāmoo)

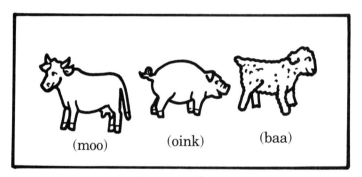

(moo)     (oink)     (baa)

(moo-oinkbaa)

Activity: Discuss the sounds made by each animal. As you point to each one, have the pupils make the animal's sound. Start slowly; then, as you speed up, stress running the animal sounds together.

**114**

4-11. Moo-Baa Blendo                                          *Auditory Sound-Blending*

| Materials: | Posterboard<br>Felt-tipped pens<br>Animal pictures<br>Construction paper<br>Paper clips<br>Glue<br>Scissors |
|---|---|
| Construction: | Make a large bingo board using a 18″×21″ piece of posterboard sectioned into 9 squares, 6″×7″ each. In each square glue or draw two or three farm animal pictures. Make calling cards of blended sounds. (See the examples.) Cut 5″ squares for markers and furnish paper clips. |

1. moo-oink          2. baaquack          3. arfoink
4. meow-arfcluck     5. meowmeow          6. neighbaa
7. gobblearf         8. cluckarf          9. baamoo-oink

| Activity: | The teacher blends the animal sounds. Based on the sound sequence, the child clips a marker over the appropriate picture. |
|---|---|

Materials:       Construction paper
Farm animal pictures
Felt-tipped pens
Clear self-stick vinyl

Construction:    Cut playing cards, 3″ × 3″. Draw or glue 1, 2, or 3 animal pictures on each card. Make one deck of 20 cards using 3 to 4 different animals in varying sequences. Cover with clear self-stick vinyl.

oinkbaacluck

oinkmoobaa

Activity:      With the teacher, pupils draw a card from the deck and blend animal sounds in the same sequence as shown. If the sounds are blended in correct order, the child keeps the card.

Materials:              Index cards, unlined, 4″ × 6″
                        Felt-tipped pens

Construction:           With bold strokes, write CV (consonant, vowel) and VC
                        (vowel, consonant) sequence combinations of known
                        letters. Mark ◿◺ below each letter for each sound to
                        be uttered separately. Mark ◯ for blended sounds.

| b,ă → bă | ă,b → ăb |
|---|---|

| c,ă → c ă | ă,c → ăc |
|---|---|

| d,ă → dă | ă,d → ăd |
|---|---|

Activity:               After some consonant and vowel sounds are known, this
                        activity may be used. Expose known consonant letters
                        with the same vowel in combination of CV then VC
                        sequence. The pupil "whispers" each separate letter
                        sound and then whisper blends the two sounds together.
                        Whispering will lessen the exaggeration of letter sounds
                        into a syllable.

4-14. Letter Talk Nonsense *Auditory Sound-Blending*

| Materials: | Index cards, unlined, $4'' \times 6''$ <br> Marking pens |
|---|---|
| Construction: | Same as #6 CVC letter sequence cards for stimulus. Do not mix vowels until all combinations of each one are mastered. |

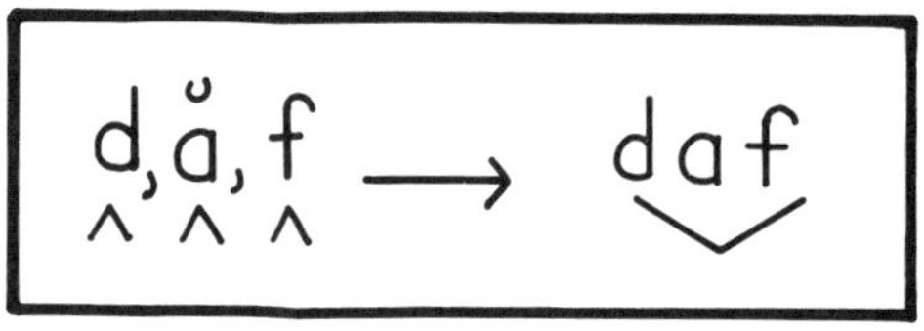

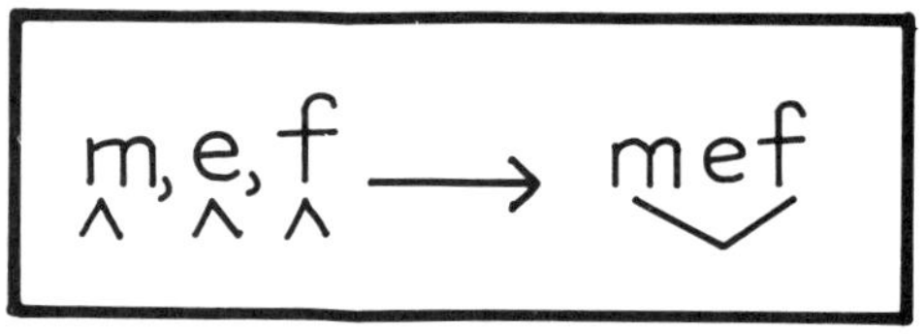

d,ă,f ⟶ daf

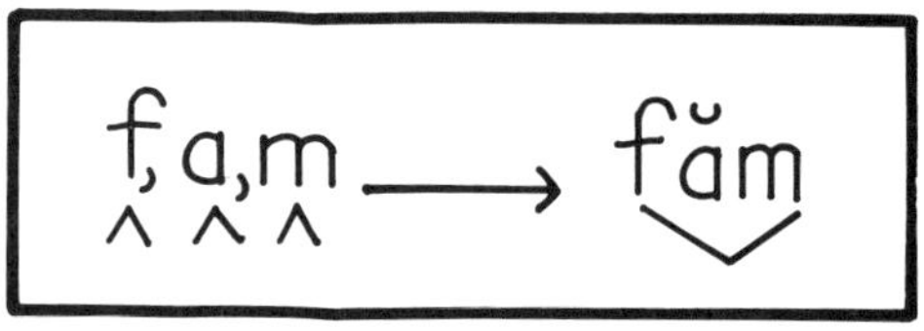

f,ă,m ⟶ făm

m,e,f ⟶ mef

| Activity: | Expose cards, one at a time, and wait for a response. Touch each ⌃ to be sounded; then, signal ⌄ for blending into a nonsense word. |

118

Name _____

Date _____

**Progress Chart**

**AUDITORY SOUND-BLENDING**

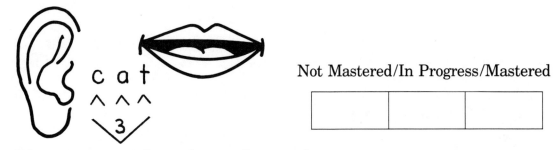

Not Mastered/In Progress/Mastered

| | | |
|---|---|---|
| | | |

I can tell how many sounds are in a spoken word.

Not Mastered/In Progress/Mastered

| | | |
|---|---|---|
| | | |

I can recognize and name letters in a word that I hear.

Not Mastered/In Progress/Mastered

| | | |
|---|---|---|
| | | |

I can name a word from sounds I hear.

Name _____

Date _____

# AUDITORY PERCEPTION SKILLS CHECKLIST

## AUDITORY FIGURE-GROUND DIFFERENTIATION

1. Listens and responds to oral commands
   while music is being played. _____

2. Recognizes and names noises that occur
   at the same time. _____

## AUDITORY DISCRIMINATION

1. Discriminates common sounds that are different. _____
2. Recognizes common sounds that are alike. _____
3. Recognizes words that rhyme. _____
4. Recognizes words that are the same. _____
5. Discriminates the word that is different. _____
6. Recognizes words that start alike. _____

## AUDITORY MEMORY AND AUDITORY SEQUENCING

1. Remembers and imitates sound patterns. _____
2. Remembers and supplies missing
   rhyming words. _____
3. Listens and retells a story. _____
4. Recalls alphabetical sequence. _____
5. Follows oral directions. _____

## AUDITORY SOUND-BLENDING

1. Distinguishes how many sounds are
   in a spoken word. _____
2. Recognizes and names letters that are
   heard in words. _____
3. Names words from sounds that are spoken. _____

| Key: | ✔ Skill mastered |
| --- | --- |
| | X Needs further instruction |

© 1987 by The Center for Applied Research in Education

# PART TWO

# Beginning to Read

The remainder of this aid will be devoted to reading readiness and to the specific reading skills a child is exposed to in grades one and two. The perceptual skills and prereadiness skills that have been discussed are all functioning together simultaneously while these reading skills are being learned and used.

Each section will include a description of specific reading skills along with examples of their uses. Activities and games that you and your students can easily make and play will be included to reinforce these skills. These activities will be followed by Progress Charts and Skills Checklists.

The skill areas that will be covered are basic reading skills (readiness), primary word attack skills (phonics and structural analysis), sight word recognition skills, and vocabulary and comprehension skills.

Also included will be three appendices containing a glossary of reading terms, sample word lists, and a resource section of other sources that can be of help to the classroom teacher.

## CHAPTER FIVE

# Building Basic Reading Skills

Reading is a complex process that requires interaction of several pre-developed skills. Reading becomes a skill development, a visual act, and a thinking process.

## THE IMPORTANCE OF THE SKILLS

When a child is attempting the task of learning to read, senses are being used, visual and auditory perceptions are interacting and the child's reactions show in various ways. He or she is relying on past experiences in order to interpret and to achieve meaning. If the young child has been experiencing a variety of pre-reading activities at home, reading success is more likely to result. If these experiences are absent, it is your obligation to provide them and fill in the gaps of readiness skill development.

The bright child who lacks certain of these abilities may have difficulty learning to read; while a slower child who has them will make progress. Just being bright is not enough when certain stages of development have been overlooked.

Reading disability is often caused by starting a child in a formal reading program before he or she is ready. If a child has had no kindergarten experience or equivalent environmental exposure, reading readiness skills must be provided in first grade before starting actual reading instruction. Some children will not be ready for reading until late in the second semester or even in the second year of school.

Reading readiness training develops finer visual and auditory discrimination skills. Probably the most basic skills are: visual letter recognition, visual discrimination of words that are the same or different, and auditory discrimination of words that rhyme and words that begin or end with the same or different sounds.

These skills may not be totally independent of one another. For example: When studying the letter recognition of *b*, the child will say the letter name, trace and write the symbol, and listen for words that begin with the same sound as *baby, boy,* or *ball*. At the same time, he or she is integrating the following abilities: visual and auditory perception, visual and auditory memory of the letter *b,* knowledge of words that start alike, and the sound of the letter that these words have in common.

## Letter Recognition

This skill sounds very simple and is often taken for granted. However, many children can sing the ABC song perfectly, but not recognize any letters past C. It is difficult for a child to remember whole words until he or she knows all of the letters, in and out of context, and whether the letters are capitals or lower case.

Remember, involvement is what makes learning stick. So, get the child involved in learning to recognize the alphabet letters.

## MATERIALS TO GATHER

File folders

Felt-tipped marking pens, assorted colors

Cardboard

Index cards, 3″ × 5″ (unlined)

Construction paper, assorted colors

Bulletin board paper, blue

Tempera paint, assorted colors

Brush, 1″

Plastic tape, assorted colors, 1″ wide

Beanbags

Large macaroni

Heavy yarn, any color

Scissors

Glue

Clear self-stick vinyl

Plastic crayon markers for transparencies

Old magazines, catalogues, or workbooks

Small boxes

Small bank envelopes or library card pockets

Small scraps of material or wallpaper

Clothespins

Fine-line felt-tipped pens, red, green, black, and blue

Pipecleaners

Clay

Raised letter blocks

ABC cereal or macaroni

Large cardboard box

Letter envelopes

Posterboard

Cookie sheet

Salt

## ACTIVITIES THAT BUILD LETTER RECOGNITION

The following activities will help develop your students' recognition of letters. Be sure the concept is understood by each student.

Materials:           One box of large macaroni
                     Fine-line felt-tipped pens, red and black
                     Heavy yarn
                     Glue

Construction:        With fine-line felt-tipped pens, write manuscript letters
                     on large macaroni. Make five of each letter, capital and
                     lower case. Consonants should be printed in black, vowels
                     in red. Dip the ends of the yarn into glue. When tacky,
                     roll them to form a permanent point.

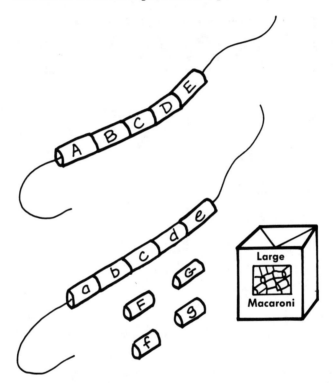

Activity:            Supply heavy yarn and a box of the lettered macaroni.
                     The pupil strings the letters of the alphabet in order onto
                     the yarn. First, string all capital letters; then, all lower
                     case letters. Later the child can pair capital and lower
                     case letters on the yarn and spell words.

Materials:         White posterboard
                   Marking pens, red, green, black, and blue
                   Plastic crayons, red, green, black, and blue
                   Clear self-stick vinyl

Construction:      Cut posterboard strips 4″ × 22″ and write manuscript
                   letters in color-coded strokes with marking pens. Cover
                   with clear self-stick vinyl. Start with 6 of the same letter
                   per card; then, 3 letters per card as shown. Make sets of
                   capital letters and small letters separately.

**1-red**
**2-green**
**3-black**
**4-blue**

Activity:          The pupil traces over each letter using the same colored
                   crayon as the color-coded stroke. Single lettered cards
                   should be practiced before tri-lettered cards are used.

Materials:    White posterboard
Marking pens, red, green, black, and blue
Plastic crayons, red, green, black, and blue
Clear self-stick vinyl

Construction:    Cut posterboard strips 4″ × 22″ and "begin" four letters per card. Complete only the first stroke. Make dots to indicate the remaining strokes in the same color coding as in activity 5-2. Cover each card with clear self-stick vinyl.

1-red                           2-green
3-black                         4-blue

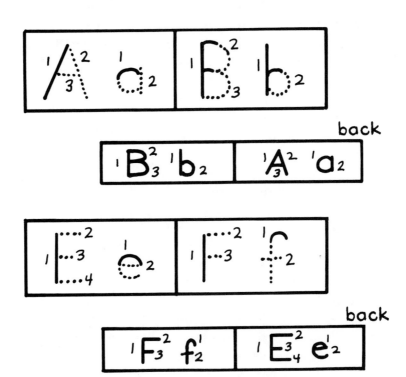

back

back

Activity:    The child is to complete each unfinished letter by connecting the dots in the same color as the writing strokes. This is training visual closure.

Materials:        Construction paper, yellow and green
                  Marking pens
                  Clear self-stick vinyl

Construction:     Make two decks of both capital and small letters on
                  construction paper cards, 2½″ × 3″. On one edge, make a
                  ¼″ black border. This signifies the bottom edge so that
                  the letters will be placed right side up. Cover the cards
                  with clear self-stick vinyl.

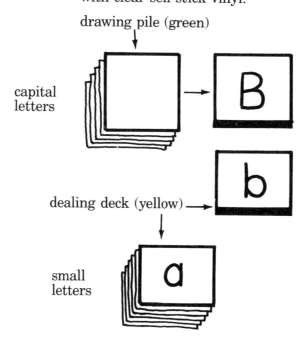

Activity:         The letters being studied are dealt out to 2 to 4 players
                  from the yellow deck. The green deck will be the drawing
                  pile. Each child draws from this pile and lays the card
                  down so that all players can see the letter. The player
                  who has the matching letter card lays down the card,
                  names the letter, and keeps both cards. The first child to
                  use all dealt cards wins if he or she has picked up the
                  most cards.

Materials:     Cookie sheet or box lid
               Salt
               Index cards, $3'' \times 5''$
               Marking pens

Construction:  Make sample letter pattern cards with dark print on
               unlined index cards. Sprinkle salt into a box lid or cookie
               sheet.

Activity:      The child shakes the salt to spread it evenly, then traces
               the letter pattern with his finger and from memory in
               the salt. The child can refer to the pattern card for self
               checking. This is done until the correct letter formation
               is mastered.

## Visual Discrimination of Words

Each young pupil must develop the ability to recognize whether two words are the same or different. He must scrutinize the whole word from beginning to end because words like "went" and "want" are easily confused. Visual memory of letter form and sequence can be trained.

The idea of "same or different" must be well understood by the child. Activities that accomplish this must start simply and then advance into finer detailed discrimination. The first few activities given here are for pre-word discrimination to help teach the meaning of "same" and "different."

After a lot of time is spent comparing and grouping or matching similar objects or pictures, the activities can be refined. Patterns drawn with more detail can be introduced. Letters can be compared as same and different. Then, when the child has an understanding of the process, whole words can be presented together or paired.

## MATERIALS TO GATHER

(See the list given under "Letter Recognition.")

## ACTIVITIES THAT BUILD
## VISUAL DISCRIMINATION OF WORDS

The following activities will help develop your students' visual discrimination of words. Be sure the concept is understood by each student.

Materials:          Construction paper, assorted colors
                    Posterboard
                    Small storage boxes
                    Scissors
                    Felt-tipped pens

Construction:       Cut posterboard into 8″ × 8″ squares and line off into 4″
                    squares. Also, cut posterboard strips 8″ × 4″ and half with
                    felt-tipped pen. This strip will contain only two squares.
                    On the strips draw a large shape in each square. On the
                    large 8″ × 8″ boards, draw four basic shape patterns. Out
                    of construction paper, cut several sizes and colors of each
                    basic shape. Store these in the box.

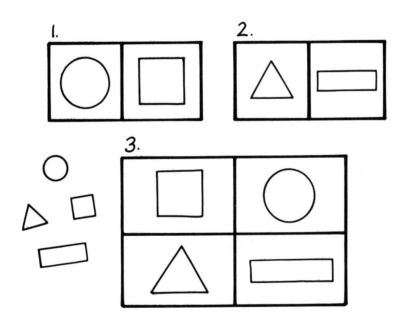

Activity:           Using the two-squared boards first, the pupil matches
                    the same shape to the drawn pattern regardless of size or
                    color. Later, he uses the four-squared board in order to
                    increase difficulty.

Materials:     Posterboard
               Index cards
               Construction paper
               Scissors
               Marking pens

Construction:  Cut posterboard into 9″ × 12″ sections. With marking pens, divide each section into six rows. On each row, write manuscript letters. Make all but one the same. On index cards or construction paper, write manuscript letters that match the "different" letter in each row. On the back, attach an envelope to store loose letters.

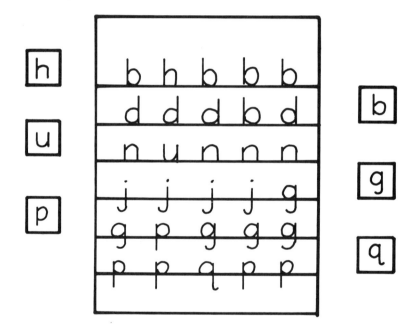

Activity:      The pupil removes the loose letters and matches the letter cards to each letter that is "different" in each row.

Materials:              Construction paper
                        Marking pens
                        Clear self-stick vinyl or plastic sheets
                        Plastic crayons

Construction:           Line off rows on a 9″ × 12″ piece of construction paper.
                        With marking pen, write four words in each row, three of
                        which are alike. The first set of cards should contain
                        words that are visually very different. Later ones may
                        contain words that are very alike in shape and number of
                        letters.

a.

| and | and | for | and |
| for | we | for | for |
| one | the | the | the |
| one | two | one | one |

b.

| in | on | on | on |
| was | saw | was | was |
| bend | hand | bend | bend |
| want | want | went | want |

Activity:               The pupil is to circle all words in each row that are
                        exactly alike. The board can be wiped with dry cloth and
                        reused.

Materials:    Construction paper
              Marking pens
              Small envelopes

Construction:  On a piece of construction paper, $12'' \times 18''$, draw Willie
               Worm. In each body section write a word that is being
               studied. Cut small word cards from the same
               construction paper. Make a word card for each word on
               the body. Glue a small envelope pocket above the head in
               which to store the word cards.

Activity:    The pupil removes the word cards from the pocket. He or
             she is to compare the words on the cards with the words
             on the body sections. Each word card is to be laid on the
             correct matching word.

## Auditory Discrimination of Words and Sounds in Words

The ability to discriminate auditorily between sounds determines whether or not a child can learn phonetic word attack skills. He or she must be able to hear rhyming words and to distinguish between words that are the same or begin or end with the same sound.

Start with simple activities and move slowly to the more complex. Readiness activities for pre-word auditory discrimination are given in the section on *Auditory Perception*. Therefore, the activities for auditory discrimination of words and sounds in words will be presented as a list. These can be used in groups or with the entire class and do not require materials. All activities are for listening and answering.

1. Read rhymes to your pupils. Have the children listen for words that rhyme and repeat them.

2. Read familiar rhymes, leaving out each rhyming word. Let the children supply the missing rhyming word as you read.

3. Produce clapping patterns. Have the children tell if the patterns were the same or different.

   | | |
   |---|---|
   | a. 2 claps (fast) | b. 4 steady claps |
   | 3 claps (slow)    different | 4 steady claps    same |

4. Ask the children to listen to three words. Have them repeat the two words that are exactly the same, but do not refer to them as rhyming words (bear, bat, bear, for example).

5. Ask the children to listen closely to the beginning sounds only. At first, all words should start alike.

6. After a while, ask the children to listen to three words, then four. Have a child repeat the words that start alike.

   | | | | |
   |---|---|---|---|
   | *car* | dog | *c*at | |
   | *dog* | *deer* | house | *dot* |

7. This is similar to number five but the child is to listen for the same ending sound. At first all words will end the same.

   | | | |
   |---|---|---|
   | ca*t* | nigh*t* | hu*t* |
   | ha*d* | sai*d* | di*d* |

8. Now, the child repeats words that end alike.

   | | | | |
   |---|---|---|---|
   | ca*t* | dog | nigh*t* | |
   | ho*g* | make | di*g* | bu*g* |

9. Now the children are ready to produce the words that start alike. Ask them to look around the room. "Can you seen anything that starts like baby?" (book, boy, ball, for example). Make sure that something is visible that does start with the same sound as your stimulus word.

These activities will sharpen auditory awareness of sounds and the placement of sounds in words. Notice that no mention has been made of the letter name for each sound. When these activities are mastered, the children will be ready to begin exercises emphasizing phonetic word attack skills and symbol-sound relationships which are covered in the next section on *Primary Word Attack Skills*.

Name _____

Date _____

Progress Chart

## BEGINNING READING SKILLS

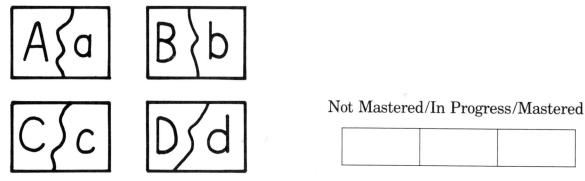

Not Mastered/In Progress/Mastered

| | | |
|---|---|---|
| | | |

I recognize and can match alphabet letters.

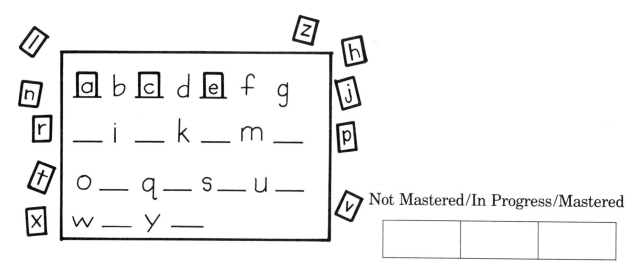

Not Mastered/In Progress/Mastered

| | | |
|---|---|---|
| | | |

I can supply any missing letters in a sequence.

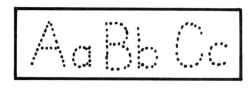

Not Mastered/In Progress/Mastered

| | | |
|---|---|---|
| | | |

Using a pattern, I can copy the alphabet letters.

Name _____

Date _____

**Progress Chart**

**BEGINNING READING SKILLS**
(continued)

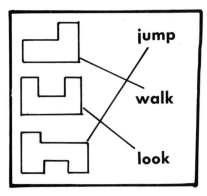

I can match word shapes with the correct words.

Not Mastered/In Progress/Mastered

| | | |
|---|---|---|
| | | |

| | | | |
|---|---|---|---|
| *and* | here | *and* | go |
| *for* | go | *for* | the |
| it | *the* | to | *the* |

I can find words that are alike.

Not Mastered/In Progress/Mastered

| | | |
|---|---|---|
| | | |

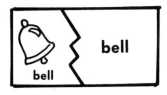

I can match words to picture-word cards.

Not Mastered/In Progress/Mastered

| | | |
|---|---|---|
| | | |

Name _____

Date _____

Progress Chart

## BEGINNING READING SKILLS
### (continued)

"Humpty Dumpty sat on a *wall*.
Humpty Dumpty had a great *fall*."

Not Mastered/In Progress/Mastered

| | | |
|---|---|---|
| | | |

I can recognize and repeat rhyming words.

| | | |
|---|---|---|
| *b*aby | *b*at | cat |
| ca*t* | go | ligh*t* |

Not Mastered/In Progress/Mastered

| | | |
|---|---|---|
| | | |

When I listen well, I can recognize words that start and end alike.

Name _____

Date _____

## BEGINNING READING SKILLS CHECKLIST

### LETTER RECOGNITION

1. Recognizes and matches alphabet letters, capital to lower case. _____

2. Supplies missing letters in the alphabetical sequence. _____

3. Copies the letters of the alphabet, using a pattern. _____

### VISUAL DISCRIMINATION OF WORDS

1. Matches word shapes to the correct words. _____

2. Finds words that are alike. _____

3. Matches words to picture-word cards. _____

### AUDITORY DISCRIMINATION OF WORDS AND SOUNDS IN WORDS

1. Recognizes and repeats rhyming words. _____

2. Recognizes words that start and end with the same sound. _____

| Key: | ✔ Skill mastered |
|------|------------------|
|      | X Needs further instruction |

## CHAPTER SIX

# Building Primary Word Attack Skills

When the pupil can recognize letters by sight and auditorily distinguish words that start alike, he or she is usually ready to begin work on the word attack skills.

These skills are merely tools for the child to develop and to use when approaching an unknown word. It would be a laborious chore for a child to have to be told every word he sees rather than to have a means by which he can decide for himself.

When word attack instruction begins, other reading skills are also being learned. The child is not just decoding words (breaking words apart) for the purpose of blending them back together. He is also learning sight words so that what he does learn to decode can be used in context and become more meaningful and useful. After all, understanding what the words are "saying" is one of the most important aspects of learning to read.

However, to help you work on the specific skills your pupils need, these skills will be discussed separately. Definitions and examples will be given along with practice activities. If you are a first grade teacher, you should know what skills are taught in grade two. If you are a second grade teacher, you should know what your pupils were exposed to in grade one. This will help to assure continuity of skill instruction from one level to another with less chance of overlooking skill gaps.

A word of caution. Please don't take this as a list of skills to immediately "run the class through." Use these activities as reinforcement when these skills are being introduced in your reading program.

Word attack skills fall into two categories: phonics (letter sounds) and structural analysis (parts of words).

## THE IMPORTANCE OF PHONICS SKILLS

Phonics, or symbol/sound relationships, is the association of a letter name with a particular sound, such as the letter "b" heard in *b*aby, *b*oy, *b*ox, *b*ear, and so on.

Sounds of consonants are more consistent, therefore we begin with these, applying auditory discrimination. Only when the child can hear and distinguish similarities and differences of the beginning sounds in words is he or she ready to try visually to associate a letter with that sound. The child needs to hear and recognize the same sounds in different locations; for example, the initial sound "b" in *b*oy, the medial sound of "b" in ri*bb*on, and, the final sound of "b" in ca*b*.

## Consonant Blends and Digraphs

The study of other beginning consonant sounds that follow single consonants are consonant blends and digraph.

Consonant blends are combinations of two consonants with both letter sounds pronounced; such as "cl" in *cl*ock and "fr" in *fr*og. The consonant blends studied in grades one and two are: bl__, br__, cl__, cr__, dr__, fl__, fr__, gl__, gr__, pl__, pr__, sc__, sk__, sl__, sm__, sn__, sp__, st__, and tr__. Ending consonant blend sounds are: __nk, __ng, __nd, __nt, and __mp.

Consonant digraphs are two consonants that exhibit a different sound when written together. For example: *th*em . . . "th" is the consonant digraph that does not make the sound of "t" or the sound of "h", but does make the sound as heard at the beginning of *th*at, *th*ose, *th*in, and *th*ey. The consonant digraphs studied in grades one and two are: th__, ch__, wh__, and sh__, as in *th*em, *ch*ain, *wh*eel, and *sh*ow.

## VOWELS

Vowels are also introduced at this time. These sounds are less consistent because, unlike most consonant letters, the vowels represent two or more sounds. Also, there is more difficulty in auditorily distinguishing vowel sounds in the middle position of the word. Therefore, in early vowel instruction, short vowels are usually presented in three letters words containing a constant element. The constant unchanged element is called a "word family" and only the beginning consonant is substituted (consonant substitution). For example: the "at" family includes b*at*, c*at*, f*at*, h*at*, m*at*, and the like. In this manner, the student can build a large number of sight words quickly. This is very encouraging to the beginner and activities can be developed to reinforce this skill. Young children soon discover the rhyming part and like to develop "silly stories" using words that rhyme.

The word families in reading for short vowel study are:

ă . . . at (hat), ag (bag), ack (sack), and (hand).

ĕ . . . en (hen), et (let), eg (leg), ed (red).

ĭ . . . it (bit), in (pin), ig (pig).

ŏ . . . og (dog), ock (sock), ot (hot).

ŭ . . . ug (rug), un (sun), ump (jump)

Long vowel study can be started with word families and consonant substitution, also. For example: a long "a" word family such as *ake* will include bake, cake, lake, make, and rake. Some word families for long vowel study are:

ā . . . ake (bake), ale (whale).

ī. . . ike (like), ight (light).

ō . . . ose (nose), old (hold).

Refer to appendix B for other suggested words to use at this level of instruction.

## Vowel Spelling Patterns

Spelling patterns can be introduced after consonant substitution and word families are studied. These skills make the child aware of a visual sequence of letters that determine pronunciation. In the sequence, the abbreviations are C (consonant), and V (vowel). The word *hat* has the sequence of consonant-vowel-consonant and a short vowel sound. Therefore, CVC is the spelling pattern.

One long vowel word family pattern is consonant-vowel-consonant-silent e, or CVCȼ (/ indicates silence). Words such as *māke* and *nōse* follow this spelling pattern.

Another spelling pattern exhibiting a long vowel sound is consonant-long vowel-silent vowel-consonant sequence; or, CVⱽC. Words that follow this pattern are: *pail, rain, sheep,* and *boat.* These combinations are known as vowel digraphs.

## Other Vowel Combinations

Vowel diphthongs and vowel-r controlled combinations are also introduced in the early grades. Diphthongs are vowel combinations such as *ow, ou, oi, oy, aw,* and *oo.* They can be practiced in the same manner as described in the word families. Picture words that help students with these combinations are: clown, house, coin, boy, paw, moon, and book.

Vowel sounds are changed when followed by the consonant "r." Thus, words containing the combination of "vowel-r" can be reinforced in the same manner as suggested, using key pictures and CVr tachistoscopes. This is most effective because of the manipulative factor. Key pictures for this pattern are: barn, bird, fur, and fern. The vowel and "r" could be written in red, the consonants in black for contrast.

## THE IMPORTANCE OF STRUCTURAL ANALYSIS SKILLS

Structural analysis simply means studying or analyzing specific word parts. These skills include adding word endings to form plurals and change tense, adding syllables, and creating compound words and contractions.

## Endings

The first ending skill is probably adding "s" to picture words to denote "more than one." The young reader is also learning number words that are used with the picture words, such as, one ball and two balls. Later the student learns to form plurals by adding "es" to singular words ending in "s" . . . buses; "x" . . . foxes; "ch" . . . benches; and "sh" . . . dishes.

Then, as sight words are built and ideas are expanded in oral communication, endings such as "ed" and "ing" can be used. The usage of these words will develop understanding of *tense* changes in context. For example: I play ball. Yesterday, I played ball. Right now, I am playing ball.

By second grade, children learn to add and use endings such as y, ly, er, and est.

## Syllables

While the study of endings progresses, the idea of "number" of syllables or word parts is introduced.

Adding "s" does not add a syllable. *Play* and *plays* contains only one syllable. However, adding "ing" or "es" will add a syllable; such as in play and playing, bus and buses. Adding "ed" sometimes adds a syllable; but, only if the "e" is heard; such as, handed. In words such as looked, played, and rained, there is only one syllable.

A way to begin teaching this discrimination is to have the young child clap word parts as the words are read by the teacher or parent. Children are attuned to rhythm and pick up the idea of "feeling" word parts quickly. For example: playing . . . clap on "play" . . . clap on "ing."

## Compound Words

Compound words are two words combined to form one word; such as, foot and ball—football. This is another word-building skill that also develops syllabication. Learning this skill should begin in grade one and be expanded in grade two.

## Contractions

Recognizing contractions is another structural analysis skill studied in grades one and two. Contractions are also formed by putting two words together. However, when forming these new words, one or more letters will be omitted and an apostrophe inserted; that is, cannot becomes can't.

### MATERIALS TO GATHER

| | |
|---|---|
| Unlined cards, $3'' \times 5''$ | Construction paper, assorted colors |
| Felt-tipped pens, assorted colors | Yarn |
| Workbooks or catalogues | Heavy paper plates |
| Scissors | Pizza boards |
| Glue | Wooden clothespins |
| Posterboard, assorted colors | Clear self-stick vinyl |

### ACTIVITIES THAT BUILD WORD ATTACK SKILLS

The following activities will help develop your students' word attack skills. Be sure the concept is understood by each student.

Materials:            Report folders with brads, one per child
                      Old catalogues
                      Construction paper, 8½″ × 11″
                      Marking pens
                      Scissors
                      Glue

Construction:         Punch two holes on the left side of 14 pages of
                      construction paper. Insert these into each folder and
                      secure with brads. Write capital and small letters in the
                      upper corner of each page and paste one picture as a
                      stimulus. Write the stimulus picture name beneath each
                      picture and underline the beginning letter.

Activity:             Each child is given a folder, scissors, glue, and catalogue
                      pictures. Pictures are found and glued to each page
                      according to the beginning sound.

Materials:         Construction paper, two colors
                   Catalogues or old workbooks
                   Scissors
                   Clear self-stick vinyl
                   Glue

Construction:      Make two decks of cards. One deck will contain a letter
                   on each card. The other will have pictures on each card.
                   On back of each picture card write the whole word and
                   underline the beginning letter.

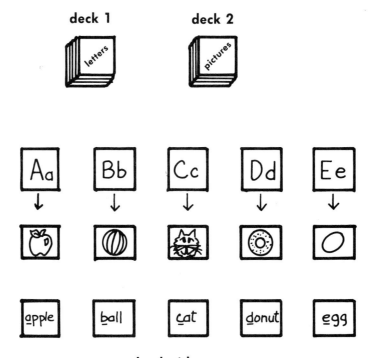

**back side**

Activity:          This game may be played like solitaire or two students
                   may play together. All letter cards are to be laid out face
                   up, in correct alphabetical sequence. The picture cards
                   are the drawing pile and should be laid picture side up.
                   As the child draws one picture card at a time, he or she
                   says the picture name and beginning sound and lays the
                   picture beside the correct letter card. The student may
                   refer to the back for self-checking.

Materials:            Heavy paper plates or pizza boards
                      Pictures from old workbooks
                      Clothespins, wooden
                      Fine-line marking pens

Construction:         Paste pictures around the rim of the paper plates or pizza
                      boards. Write the beginning letter on the back of the
                      board behind each picture. Write letters on each
                      clothespin with a marking pen.

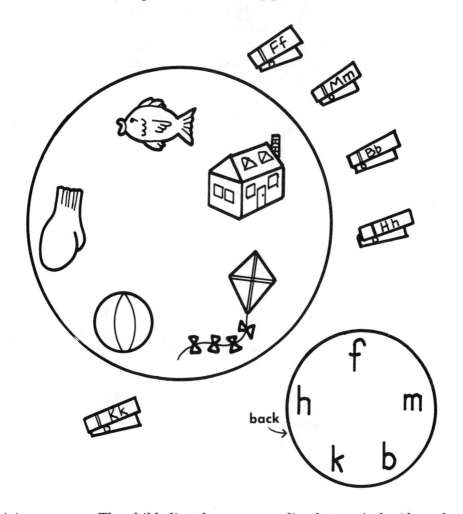

Activity:             The child clips the corresponding letter pin beside each
                      picture representing that beginning sound. He or she can
                      self-check by looking on the back of the board.

Materials:        Posterboard, 12″ × 18″
Marking pens, felt-tipped
Pictures of buildings
Scissors
Glue
Clear self-stick vinyl
Construction paper

Construction:      Make a game board as shown below. Use cut-out pictures of buildings. In each square of the road, write letters that represent the blend sounds. On construction paper cards write the numerals one through five. Cover the cards and playing board with clear self-stick vinyl. Provide discs or small objects to be used as "men" in the game.

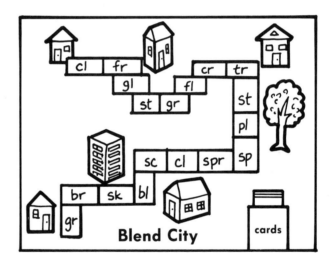

Activity:        The child draws a card for the number of moves to be taken. After the move is made, the child says a word that begins with the blend on which he or she has landed. If the incorrect word is given, the child moves back the same number of steps.

148

Materials:         Posterboard
                   Marking pens, felt-tipped
                   Clear self-stick vinyl
                   Catalogues
                   Scissors
                   Glue

Construction:      Cut strips $2'' \times 4''$ out of posterboard. Draw a line on each
                   strip to make two spaces. Write a blend in one space and
                   glue a picture that represents a blend on the other side.
                   See the Sample Word Lists of Blends and Digraphs for
                   suggested words. On the back side of each picture, write
                   the picture word and underline the letters that represent
                   the blend. Cover with clear self-stick vinyl.

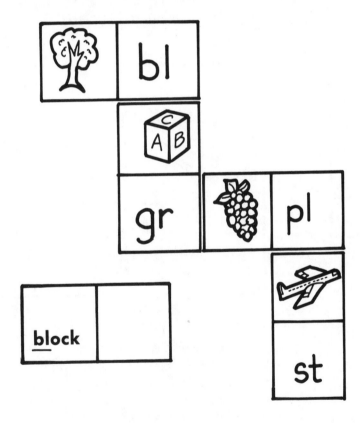

Activity:          The pictures are to be matched to the correct blend by
                   playing a domino-type game. This may be done alone or
                   with a buddy.

Materials:        Posterboard, 12″ × 18″
                  Marking pens, felt-tipped
                  Construction paper, assorted colors
                  Scissors
                  Glue
                  Large lima beans, 4
                  Clear self-stick vinyl

Construction:     Make a game board as shown below. Each square in the
                  road is a 1″ piece of construction paper cut from different
                  colors and glued to the board. On each square in the
                  road, write the letters that represent different digraph
                  sounds. On construction paper cards write numerals one
                  through five. Cover the cards and game board with clear
                  self-stick vinyl. Paint the lima beans red, blue, green,
                  and orange with marking pens.

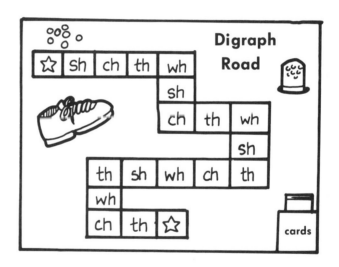

Activity:         The pupil draws a card for the number of moves to be
                  taken. At each landing, the child gives a word that begins
                  with the digraph in that square. If he or she is unable to
                  give a word, the turn is lost. A similar board can be
                  made for ending sounds.

Materials: Posterboard
Marking pens, felt-tipped
Clear self-stick vinyl
Catalogues
Scissors
Glue

Construction: Cut 2″ × 4″ strips out of posterboard. With marking pen, draw a vertical line to divide each strip. One one side, write a digraph. On the other side, glue a picture that represents a digraph sound. See appendix B for suggested words. On the back side of each picture, write the picture word and underline the letters that represent the digraph. Cover with clear self-stick vinyl.

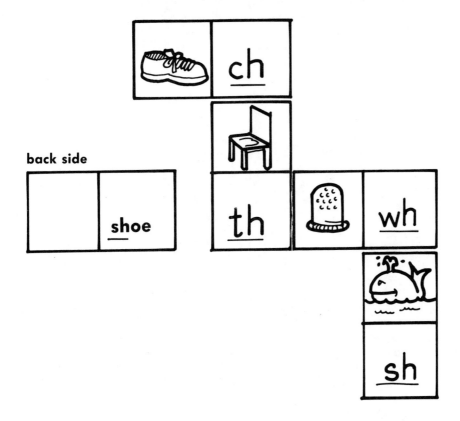

Activity: The pictures are to be matched to the correct blend by playing a domino-type game. This may be done alone or with a buddy.

Materials:        Construction paper
Catalogues
Scissors
Glue

Construction:     Make one page for each consonant digraph and consonant blend to be added to the pictionary. Write the digraph or blend letters in the upper left corner and glue one picture that represents that sound on each page.

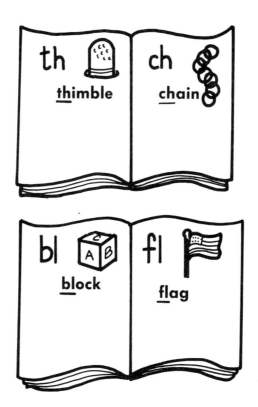

Activity:        Pupils find pictures beginning with each consonant digraph or blend and glue these to the correct page.

Materials:        Posterboard, $7'' \times 9''$
Marking pens, red and black
Scissors
Clear self-stick vinyl

Construction:     Refer to the List of Word Families to select picture
patterns. Draw a stimulus picture, such as hat, on the
posterboard and cut the outline. Make a word strip
$1\frac{1}{2}'' \times 10''$. On the strip write words that contain the word
family. The family phoneme letters are to be written in
red, the other letters in black. Cut two slits $1\frac{5}{8}''$ wide and
$\frac{1}{2}''$ apart. Insert the word strip.

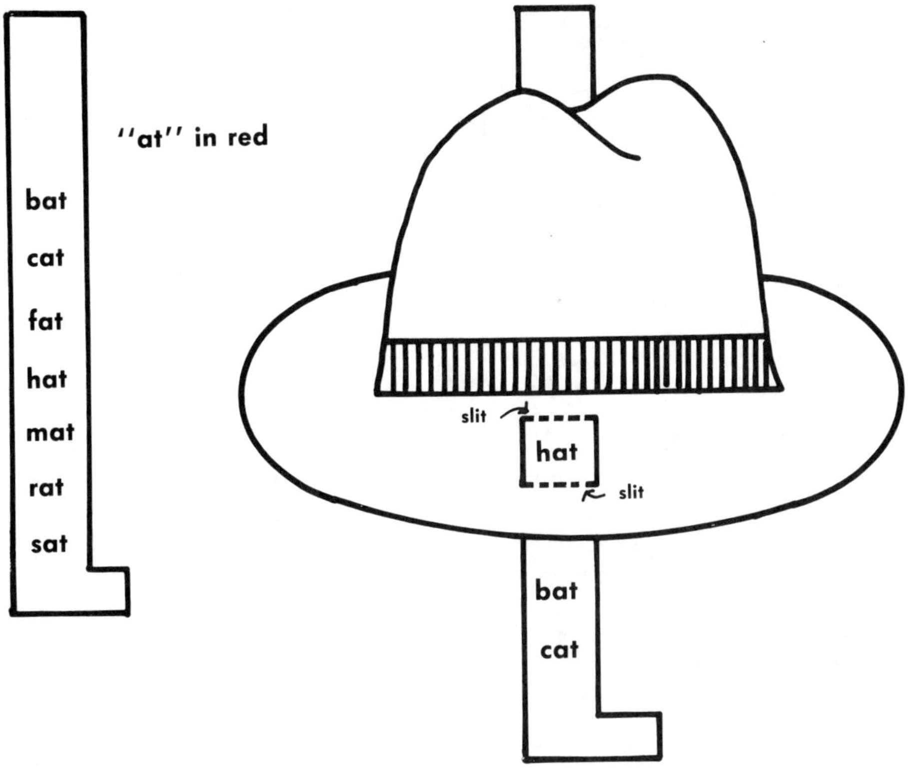

"at" in red

bat
cat
fat
hat
mat
rat
sat

slit

hat

slit

bat
cat

Activity:         Pupils move the strip up and down and read the word
exposed in the board.

Materials:           Posterboard
Marking pens, red and black
Clear self-stick vinyl
Brads

Construction:    Cut 3″ × 5″ posterboard strips. Cut discs three inches in diameter. Write the word family letters in red and cut out a one-inch window to the left of the letters. Attach the wheel discs with a brad so that one edge is exposed in the window. Write the consonants in the window in black letters. Remove the discs to cover with clear self-stick vinyl and then reassemble with the brad.

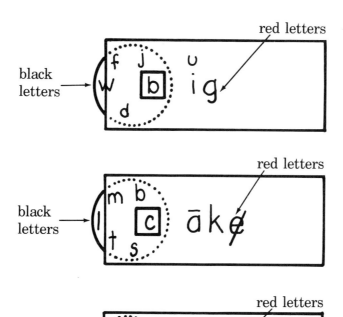

Activity:             The pupil rotates the wheel of consonant letters and reads each new word that is formed with the word family letters.

Materials:    Unlined tagboard, 4″ × 6″
              Marking pens, red and black
              Small letter cards
              Clear self-stick vinyl

Construction: Line off four rows on each card. Draw a vertical line one
              inch from the left edge and leave the left side blank.
              Write a word family phoneme to the right of the vertical
              line. Make small letter cards of consonant letters. Cover
              in clear self-stick vinyl and glue an envelope to the back
              side.

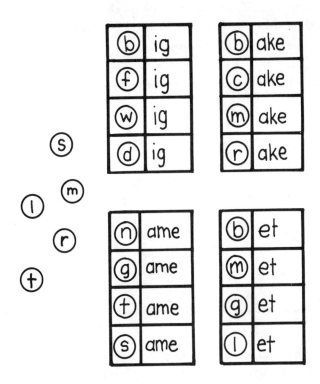

Activity:     The child uses individual letter cards to build new words
              that are formed with the existing word family.

6-12. Hit It!

Materials:       Black bulletin board paper
                 Yellow paint and brush
                 Beanbag
                 Library pocket
                 3″×5″ cards
                 Stapler

Construction:    Line off 2′×3′ bulletin board paper with yellow paint to
                 form six 12″×12″ squares. In each square paint a word
                 family. All families should contain the same vowel; such
                 as, and, an, at, ag, am, and ad. On a 3″×5″ card, write
                 words that are built with these family phonemes. Keep
                 this in a library pocket beside the game. One game board
                 should be made as each vowel is studied and new word
                 families are introduced.

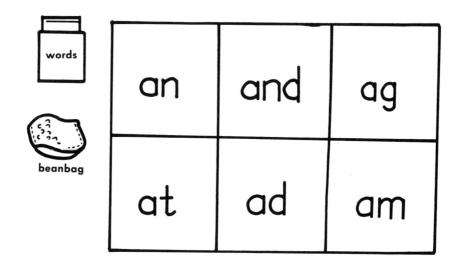

words

beanbag

| an | and | ag |
|----|-----|----|
| at | ad  | am |

Activity:        One student or teacher reads words from the card. A
                 student who is **IT** throws the beanbag to the square
                 containing the correct word family of the word read.
                 Another student is chosen and the game continues.

156

# Ideas to improve behavior

- preventive - acknowledge good beh.
- give 5 + 1 min. warnings before change of activities
- make all activities enjoyable so they want to change activity
- repeat over + over what beh. is appropriate
- give situations to role play
- discuss how we feel when...
- books on misbehavior topics
- discuss what's impt. to tell teacher vs. what isn't  eg. only tell if dangerous
- children naturally like to please adults they like so be someone they want to please
- bre dramatic when explaing appropriate beh.
- don't start activities until all are paying attn.
- small group activities when possible

class by McAllister
sub. in Kind.
my children - my sister's
teaching 4's + 5's,  ~~in Kind~~ Sun. sch - no beh. problems
childrens church 4's thru 3rd grade
class I start Tues.

## Red Cross / First Aid

reliable child care - my mother
dependable

## Activities

p. 34      Sesame Street cards
p. 59      Animal Dominoes
p. 76      Xmas card game
p. 108     Mimic
           acting out characters
           listening + giving impt. to what they say
           not paperwork
           good choices of books w/ meaning
           aide to work w/ group for activity - 3 small groups

6-13. Spell a Pattern

Materials:
Folders
Marking pens
Catalogue or workbook
Blue tagboard
Scissors
Glue
Library pockets

Construction:
On folders draw 5″×10″ two strips and divide these into one-inch squares. At the top write the word pattern (CVC, CVCͤ, CVͮC). On blue strips 3″×7″ glue pictures of words that fit these patterns. Write the words on the back. The first folders used should contain only one vowel. Later, pattern cards may contain more than one vowel. Out of the blue tagboard make small individual letter cards. Attach a pocket to hold letters. Cover with clear self-stick vinyl.

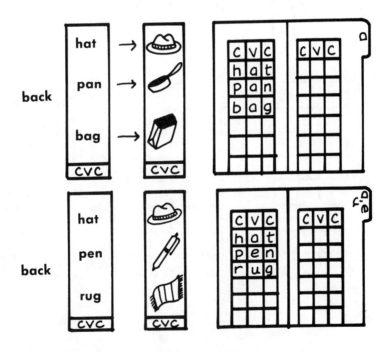

Activity:
The child is to build words that spell the picture names and fit the spelling pattern.

Materials:           Picture Dictionaries
                            Posterboard
                            Plastic marking crayons
                            Marking pens, felt-tipped
                            Clear self-stick vinyl

Construction:      Cut 5″ × 10″ posterboard strips and line off to form one-inch squares. Write the spelling pattern on the top row and one sample word. Cover with clear self-stick vinyl. Supply a Picture Dictionary and crayon to each pupil.

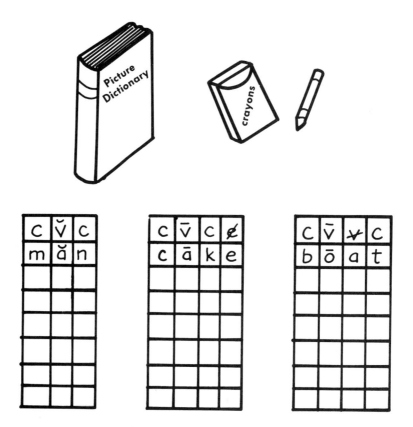

Activity:          The pupils search for picture words that fit each spelling pattern of CVC, CVCé, and CVⱽC. The words are to be copied on the pattern card as shown.

Materials:          Posterboard
                    Construction paper
                    Marking pens
                    Catalogues
                    Clear self-stick vinyl
                    Scissors
                    Glue

Construction:       Divide posterboard cards into three two-inch sections. In
                    each section write a spelling pattern such as CVC, CVCé,
                    and CVvC. Draw or glue a picture that represents each
                    pattern. Make small cards that contain pictures as
                    shown. On the back of each picture, write the pattern for
                    self-checking. Cover with clear self-stick vinyl.

pen        cat        cake       pail

Activity:           The pupil places the picture/word cards in the row that
                    contains the spelling pattern sequence of the card.

| Materials: | Posterboard<br>Marking pens<br>Unlined 3″×5″ cards<br>Envelopes<br>Clear self-stick vinyl |
| --- | --- |
| Construction: | Cut 9″×9″ posterboard squares. Line off into three-inch squares. In the squares, write the spelling pattern codes, as shown. Out of unlined cards make 1″×3″ word cards for each spelling pattern. Attach an envelope to the back of the posterboard. Cover with clear self-stick vinyl. |

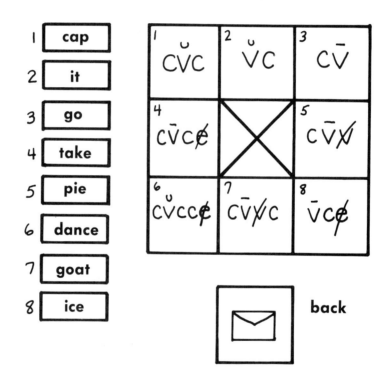

| Activity: | This activity must follow mastery of Pattern Lotto #1. The pupils remove the loose word cards and lay each card in the square that contains the same spelling pattern sequence. |
| --- | --- |

Materials:          Posterboard
                    Marking pens, red and black
                    Clear self-stick vinyl
                    Scissors

Construction:       Make posterboard tachistoscopes in the shapes of key
                    pictures. The vowel element combination should be
                    printed in red letters. See the section on Phonetic
                    Spelling Patterns and Vowel Spelling Combinations for
                    words to use. Cover with clear self-stick vinyl.

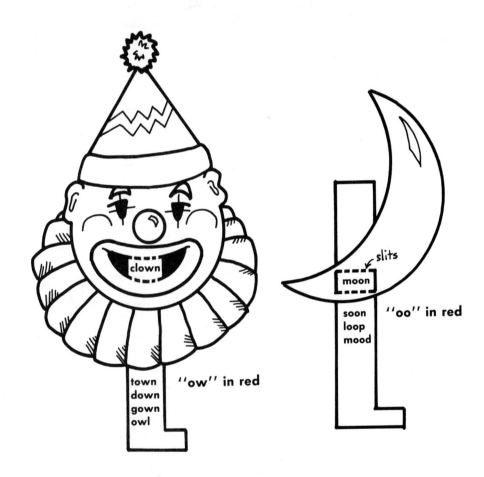

Activity:           The pupil slides the word strip and reads each word as it
                    appears in the window area.

Materials:     Posterboard
Marking pens
Scissors
Clear self-stick vinyl
Razor blade
Brads

Construction:     Cut 3″×5″ strips of posterboard. In the center of each strip, write the vowel combinations being stressed in red letters. Cut out ½″ square windows as shown. Cut 3″ circles for the discs. Write the consonants around the rims of the discs. Cover with clear self-stick vinyl and attach the discs with brads so that the consonant letters appear in the windows. Words may be written on back for self-checking.

| moon | loop |
|------|------|
| soon | loot |
| boon | boot |
| loon | mood |

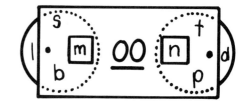

| cloud |
|-------|
| pout |
| round |
| sound |
| mound |

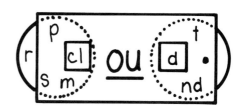

| paw | pawn |
|-----|------|
| saw | lawn |
| raw | dawn |
| claw | fawn |
|      | shawl |

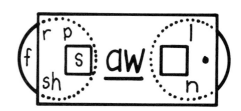

Activity:     Pupils rotate the circles and read new words that are formed by changing the beginning and ending sounds.

Materials:     Pizza boards, 8″
               Clothespins
               Fine-line marking pens
               Catalogues or old workbooks
               Scissors
               Glue
               Clear self-stick vinyl

Construction:  Around each pizza board, glue pictures that represent the
               vowel combinations being stressed. On the back side,
               write each word. On clothespins, write words for these
               pictures. The vowel element should be written in red
               letters. Cover the pizza board with clear self-stick vinyl.

Activity:      Pupils clip the correct clothespin to each picture around
               the board and read the word. The back of the wheel may
               be referred to for self-checking.

Materials: Posterboard
Marking pens, assorted colors
Scissors
Clear self-stick vinyl
Razor blade
Brads

Construction: Cut the posterboard to 3″×5″ strips. In the center write the vowel +r combination in red letters. Cut out one ½″ square window before and after the letters. Cut 3″ circles. Refer to the section of Phonetic Spelling Patterns and Vowel Spelling Combinations for words to use. Write the consonant letters around the rims of each wheel. Cover with clear self-stick vinyl. Attach wheels with brads so that the consonant letters appear in the windows. The words that are to be formed may be written on the back of the card for self-checking.

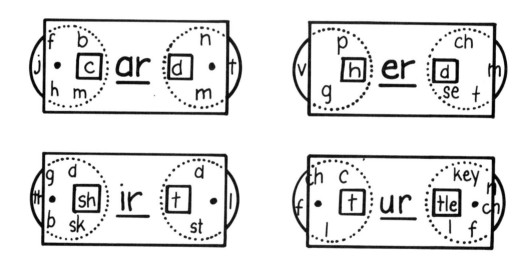

Activity: The pupil builds words by rotating the wheels and applying consonant substitution to form these new words.

Materials:        Folders
                  Marking pens, felt-tipped
                  Small individual letter cards
                  Clear self-stick vinyl

Construction:     Draw rows of unfinished words containing the vowel
                  +r phonogram only. The missing letters should be
                  designated by a blank space. Draw a picture beside each
                  word space that depicts the word that is to be completed.
                  Cover with clear self-stick vinyl. Provide small individual
                  letter cards.

Activity:         The child lays the missing consonant letters in the
                  correct blanks to complete each word.

*Plural Endings*

Materials:       Shoe box
Construction paper
Pictures of objects
Marking pens
Scissors
Glue

Construction:    Glue pictures on construction paper and write the
singular or plural form on the back. Square off the lid
and box bottom. Write the singular word in one square
and its plural form beside it. Underline the ending "s" or
"es". Store the loose picture in the shoe box.

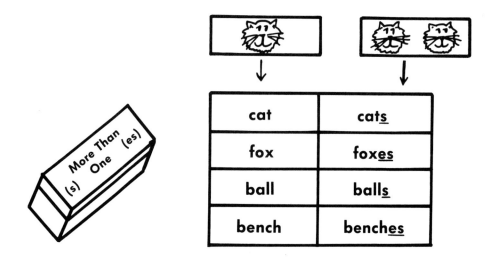

Activity:       The child removes the loose pictures from the box and
places each one in the correct word square.

Materials: Construction paper
Marking pens, felt-tipped
Catalogues
Scissors
Glue
Large brown envelope
Library pockets

Construction: Use 9″ × 12″ pieces of construction paper. Glue pictures in squares and make word cards for each picture. Write the correct word on the back side of each picture for self-checking. Glue a library pocket on the back side of each playing card to store loose words. Place the entire set in a large brown envelope for storage.

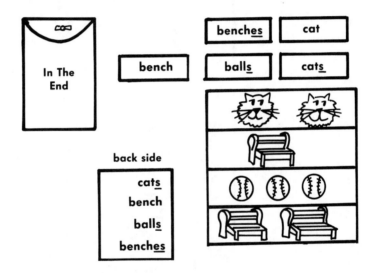

Activity: The playing cards and loose words cards are removed from the envelope and spread before the child. The pupil places the picture word card on the correct picture.

Materials:    Folders
Marking pens, felt-tipped
Catalogues
Scissors
Glue
Construction paper
Clear self-stick vinyl

Construction:    Glue pictures in rows in the folder. Beside each picture draw lines indicating how many letters the correct word contains. Make word cards of the picture words. Attach a pocket to hold the word cards. Cover with clear self-stick vinyl.

Activity:    The child places the correct word card beside each picture. The number of letters will help the child to choose the words with "s" or "es" endings.

Materials:      Folders
Marking pens, felt-tipped
Construction paper
Library pockets
Scissors

Construction:      Divide a folder into three columns with headings of Yesterday, Today, and Tomorrow. Make word cards containing words that denote tense using "ed" and "ing" endings. Include auxiliary verbs in red letters. On the back side write a sentence using the word on the card. Attach a library pocket in which to store word cards.

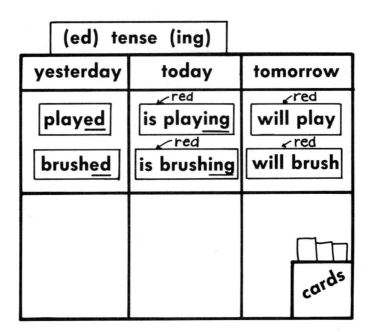

Activity:      The child removes the word cards, reads the sentence on back, and places the card in the correct column to denote tense.

Materials:         Construction paper
Fine-line marking pens or typewriter
Scissors
Clear self-stick vinyl

Construction:    Make two decks of playing cards. On one set write or type sentences with the verbs omitted. On the second set, write or type the missing words. On the back side of the sentence cards write the missing word. Cover both decks with clear self-stick vinyl.

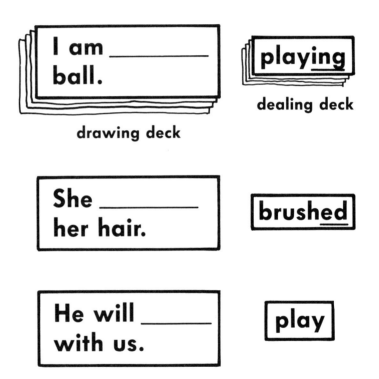

**drawing deck**

**dealing deck**

Activity:        The word cards are dealt to 2 to 4 pupils. The sentence cards are laid face up as the drawing pile. In turn, the pupils draw a sentence card. The pupil who has a word card to complete the sentence lays down the card and reads the completed form.

6-27. Box It, 1,2,3 *Syllables*

Materials:  Three boxes
Marking pens
Objects such as, hairpin, ball, tweezers, hairclip, brush,
tape, toy umbrella, ruler, timer, or glass.

Construction:  On each box write the numeral 1, 2, or 3. Beside the
numeral draw a picture of a word or object that is
composed of that number of syllables. If you cannot find
enough objects, include pictures of objects. Store these in
the boxes.

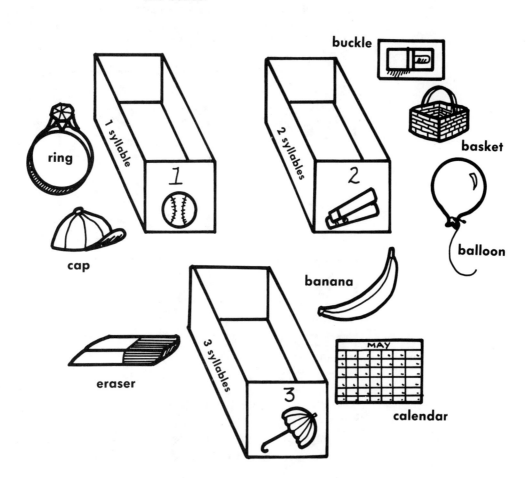

Activity:  Each item is removed from the boxes. The child gives the
name of each object, tells how many "parts" or syllables
the word contains and places the object in the box that
denotes the same number.

**171**

Materials:  Construction paper
            Catalogues
            Scissors
            Glue
            Envelopes
            Marking pens, felt-tipped
            Posterboard

Construction:  On large 12″ × 18″ posterboard, glue three envelopes. On each envelope write the numeral 1, 2, or 3. On 3″ × 3″ construction paper cards glue pictures. On the back side, write the picture name and number of syllables.

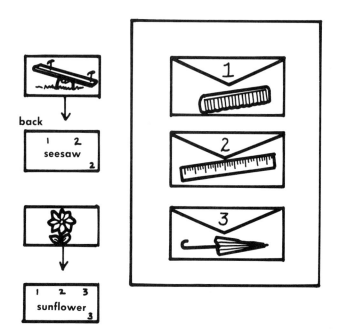

Activity:  Remove the pictures and place them before the student. The pupil places each picture in the envelope that contains the same number as the word has syllables.

Materials: Posterboard
Unlined cards, 3″ × 5″
Staples
Scissors
Marking pens, felt-tipped

Construction: Cut posterboard pieces to 7″ × 9″. Turn up one end two inches and staple the side edges down. On 3″ × 5″ cards write the numerals 1, 2, and 3. Make a set of the pocket and cards for each child in the class.

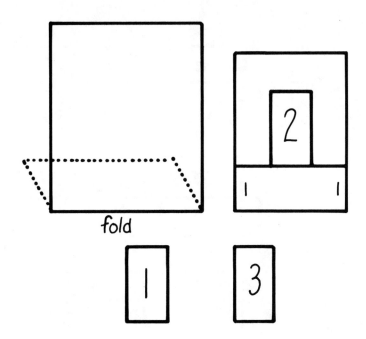

fold

Activity: Each child lays the numeral cards on the desk. The teacher reads words to the class. After each word is read, each child places the numeral that denotes the number of syllables in the pockets.

Materials:           Construction paper
                     Marking pens, felt-tipped
                     Catalogues
                     Scissors
                     Glue
                     Clear self-stick vinyl

Construction:        Use a 9″ × 12″ piece of construction paper. Turn up one end to form a pocket and staple both ends. Write large numerals in each column as shown. Glue pictures to small construction paper cards. Cover with clear self-stick vinyl.

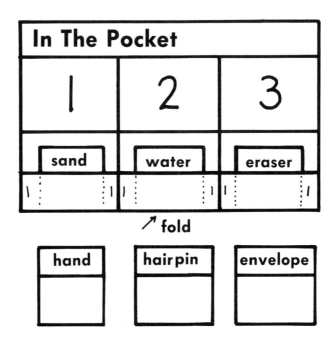

Activity:            The child removes the picture cards, names each picture, and then places the card in the pocket denoting the number of syllables in the word. Children can then play the same game using word cards.

Materials:          Unlined index cards, $3'' \times 5''$
                    Marking pens
                    Scissors
                    Clear self-stick vinyl

Construction:       Draw pictures that can be combined to build compound
                    words. Cut the two pictures apart. Write the picture
                    words beneath each picture and the compound word on
                    the back. Cover with clear self-stick vinyl.

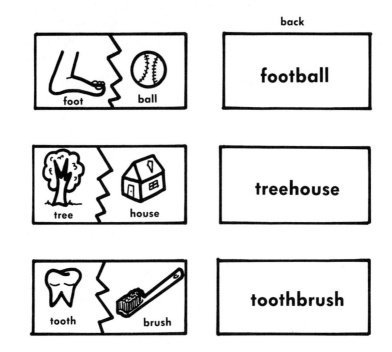

Activity:           The pupil fits the puzzles together to build compound
                    words. He or she takes the puzzles apart to exhibit the
                    two separate words that formed each compound word.

Materials:   Cardboard
             Marking pens, assorted colors
             Belt eyelets
             Eyelet tool
             Clear self-stick vinyl
             Heavy yarn or shoe strings
             Cellophane tape

Construction:   Use 9″×12″ cardboard pieces. On the left edge draw two pictures that form a compound word. On the right side write the compound word. Cover with clear self-stick vinyl paper. On each edge beside the picture and words, insert a belt eyelet. Attach a piece of knotted yarn and tape the end of each piece.

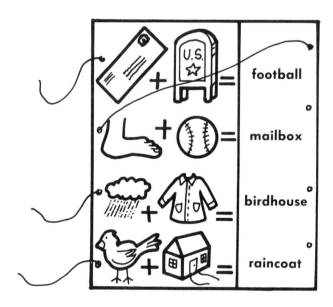

Activity:   The pupil matches the pictures to the correct compound word by inserting the yarn into the correct eyelet on the right side.

Materials:           Folders
                     Construction paper
                     Marking pens, felt-tipped
                     Scissors

Construction:        Line off the folder into two-inch rows. Draw a vertical
                     line down the middle to divide each side. In each box
                     write one compound word. On small construction paper
                     cards write the separate words that formed these
                     compounds. Attach a pocket in which to store these word
                     cards.

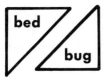
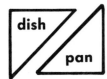
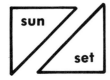

| | | | | compounds |
|---|---|---|---|---|
| **bedbug** | **cobweb** | **airplane** | **dishpan** | |
| **bulldog** | **into** | **pigpen** | **popgun** | |
| **wigwag** | **daylight** | **sunset** | **tomcat** | |
| **backbone** | **milkman** | **eyebrow** | **night** **nighttime** **time** | |

Activity:            The pupil removes all loose word cards and then places
                     them in the box that contains the correct compound
                     word.

Materials:          Construction paper
                    Marking pens or typewriter
                    Scissors
                    Clear self-stick vinyl

Construction:       Cut construction paper cards 3″×5″ and 2″×3″. On the
                    3″×5″ cards write or type unfinished riddles as shown.
                    On the smaller cards write or type the missing compound
                    words. On the back of each riddle card, write the missing
                    compound word for self-checking. Cover with clear self-
                    stick vinyl.

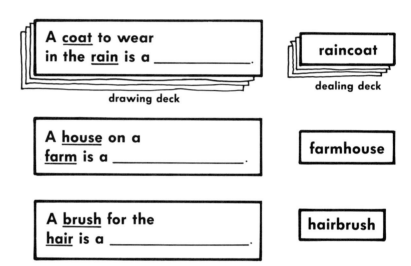

Activity:           Place the riddle cards face up before the children and
                    then deal compound cards to 2 to 4 pupils. In turn, the
                    children draw a riddle card and the pupil who has the
                    compound word card lays it down. Play continues until
                    all cards are used.

Materials:            Unlined newsprint
                      Felt-tipped pens
                      Scissors

Construction:         On strips of unlined paper, write two words that will
                      form the new contractions that are being introduced.
                      Supply these word strips and a pair of scissors to each
                      child.
                      For each set make small cards each containing an
                      apostrophe.

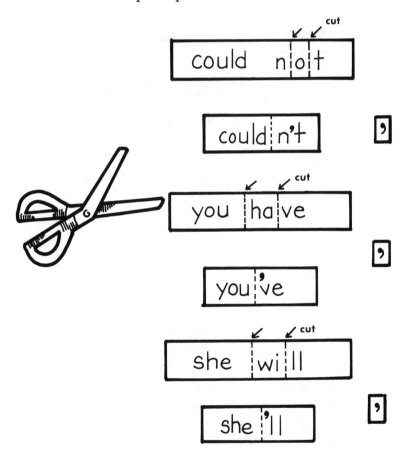

Activity:             To help the children remember which letters are to be
                      removed in order to form contractions, have each child
                      cut away these letters and replace them with an
                      apostrophe card.

Materials:          Tagboard
                    Felt-tipped pens
                    Envelopes, $4'' \times 6''$

Construction:       Cut $3'' \times 7''$ tagboard strips. On these, write the two words
                    that will form contractions. With lines, enclose the letters
                    that need to be omitted when forming a contraction.
                    Write the contraction on the back. Make small letter
                    cards and several cards containing an apostrophe. Place
                    the cards and letters in the envelopes.

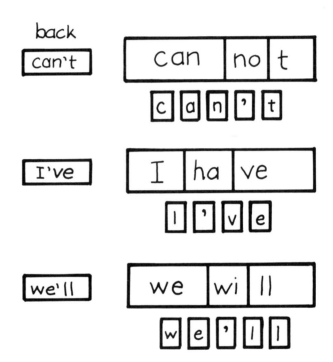

Activity:           The child removes all cards and letters. Beneath each
                    card containing the two words, the child uses small letter
                    cards to build the contraction. The child may then refer
                    to the back of the strip for self-checking.

Materials:    Pizza boards
              Clothespins, wooden
              Fine-line marking pens
              Clear self-stick vinyl

Construction: With marking pen, divide the pizza board into sections.
              Write double words in each section. On the clothespins,
              write corresponding contractions. Cover the pizza board
              with clear self-stick vinyl.

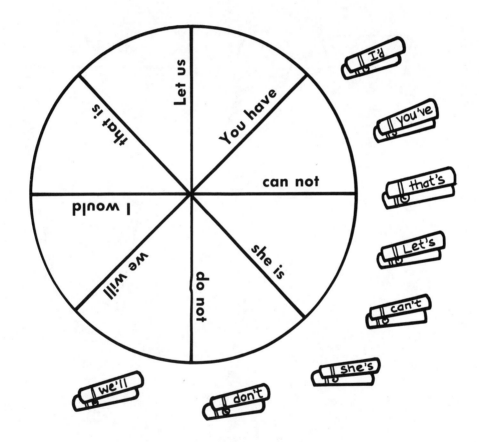

Activity:     The pupil matches the contraction to each set of double
              words by clipping the corresponding clothespin to the
              correct section.

Materials:        Brown construction paper
                  Yellow and orange construction paper
                  Felt-tipped pens
                  Scissors

Construction:     Using this pattern, cut cones out of brown paper and
                  scoops of ice cream out of yellow and orange paper. Write
                  the contraction and a sentence on each cone. Write the
                  two words that form the contraction on the ice cream.

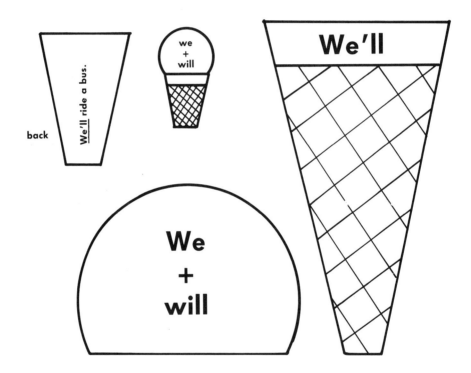

Activity:         The pupil matches the scoop of ice cream to the correct
                  cone. To keep the cone, the child must read the sentence
                  on the back.

Materials:          Posterboard
                    Marking pens
                    Scissors
                    Clear self-stick vinyl

Construction:       Cut two decks of cards; one 3″ × 5″ and one 2″ × 3″. On the
                    3″ × 5″ cards write sentences using contractions.
                    Underline each contraction word. On the smaller cards,
                    write the two words that formed each contraction used.
                    Cover with clear self-stick vinyl.

Activity:           The drawing pile will consist of cards that contain
                    sentences. Deal the word cards to 2 to 4 players. In turn,
                    each child draws a sentence card and reads it aloud. Any
                    player having the correct word card can play it. The
                    game continues until all cards are used.

Name —————————————————

Date —————————————————

## Progress Chart

## PRIMARY WORD ATTACK SKILLS

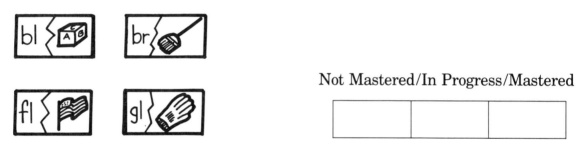

Not Mastered/In Progress/Mastered

| | | |
|---|---|---|
| | | |

I can correctly match consonant letters to pictures beginning with those sounds.

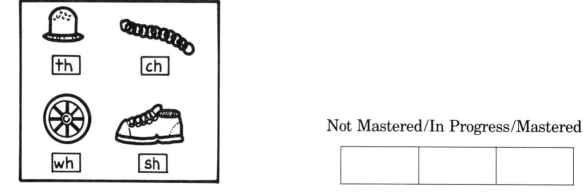

Not Mastered/In Progress/Mastered

| | | |
|---|---|---|
| | | |

I can correctly match blends puzzles by correctly associating the blends sounds with pictures.

Not Mastered/In Progress/Mastered

| | | |
|---|---|---|
| | | |

I can distinguish different consonant digraphs by matching digraph cards (sh, ch, th, or wh) to the correct pictures.

Name _____

Date _____

**Progress Chart**

## PRIMARY WORD ATTACK SKILLS
### (continued)

| | |
|---|---|
| _at | _en |
| _og | _et |
| _ish | _ike |
| _ake | _ame |

Not Mastered/In Progress/Mastered

| | | |
|---|---|---|
| | | |

When playing Family Bingo, I can correctly locate the word family part of each spoken word.

| c v̆ C | c v̄ c¢ | c v̄ v̸ c |
|---|---|---|
| hat | rake | rain |
| pig | name | beat |
| hen | rose | coat |

Not Mastered/In Progress/Mastered

| | | |
|---|---|---|
| | | |

I can match word cards to the correct spelling patterns of CVC, CVC¢, or CVv̸C.

town
gown

Not Mastered/In Progress/Mastered

| | | |
|---|---|---|
| | | |

I can read words containing vowel diphthongs (ow, ou, oi, oy, aw, or oo) on tachistoscope strips.

Name ————————————————————

Date ————————————————————

Progress Chart

PRIMARY WORD ATTACK SKILLS
(continued)

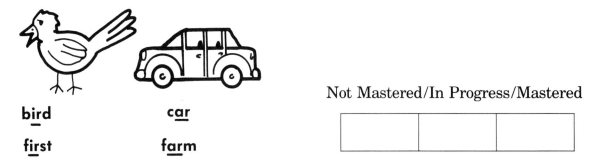

Not Mastered/In Progress/Mastered

| | | |
|---|---|---|
| | | |

I recognize and can match "r" controlled words to the correct pictures.

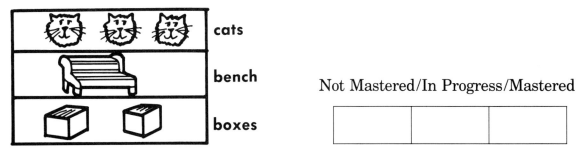

Not Mastered/In Progress/Mastered

| | | |
|---|---|---|
| | | |

I recognize singular and plural forms of nouns.

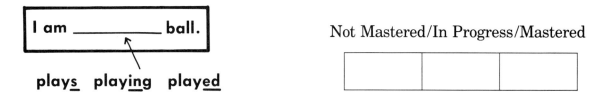

Not Mastered/In Progress/Mastered

| | | |
|---|---|---|
| | | |

I recognize and use inflected verb endings (s, ed, and ing) by using the correct word card in incomplete sentences.

Name _____

Date _____

Progress Chart

## PRIMARY WORD ATTACK SKILLS
### (continued)

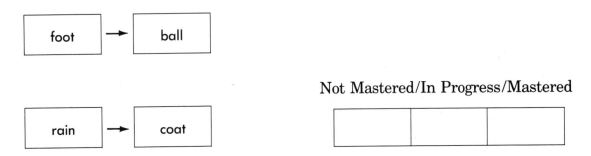

"plays"      1

(clap)

Not Mastered/In Progress/Mastered

"playing"    2

(clap) (clap)

I can "clap" word parts and determine the correct number of syllables.

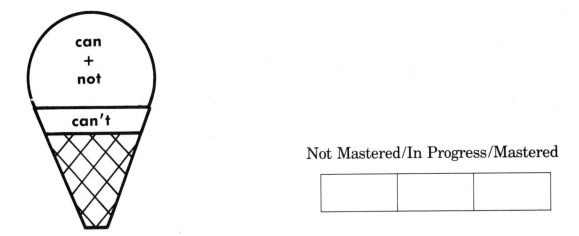

foot → ball

Not Mastered/In Progress/Mastered

rain → coat

I can recognize and pair word cards to form compound words.

can
+
not

can't

Not Mastered/In Progress/Mastered

I can match contractions to the words that form these contractions.

Name _____

Date _____

## PRIMARY WORD ATTACK SKILLS CHECKLIST

### PHONICS

1. Matches pictures to beginning sounds, single consonants.
2. Matches pictures to beginning consonant blend sounds.                    _____
3. Recognizes consonant digraph sounds.                    _____
4. Recognizes word family parts.                    _____
5. Recognizes and uses spelling patterns.                    _____
6. Recognizes and applies the vowel diphthong sounds.                    _____
7. Correctly applies "r" control to vowel sounds.                    _____

### STRUCTURAL ANALYSIS

1. Recognizes singular and plural forms of nouns.                    _____
2. Correctly uses inflected verb endings.                    _____
3. Determines the correct number of syllables in words.                    _____
4. Recognizes and forms compound words.                    _____
5. Recognizes and forms contractions.                    _____

| Key: | ✔ Skill mastered |
| --- | --- |
| | X Needs further instruction |

© 1987 by The Center for Applied Research in Education

## CHAPTER SEVEN

# Building Sight Word Recognition Skills

As mentioned before, phonics and structural analysis will become tools a child uses when he or she encounters new words. After the new words are decoded and pronounced, however, word meaning is not an automatic outcome. Without understanding the meanings of these words, the process of decoding becomes mere word naming.

The ultimate goal of all this effort is for the child to understand what he reads. Reading then becomes a meaningful activity that will be a lifetime companion. After all, reading is breaking the code of graphic symbols and interpreting what an author intended to say. It is the message in the words that must be the end product for the reader.

## THE IMPORTANCE OF THE SKILL

Sight word recognition is the ability to know a word, instantly, when one sees it. That is not as easy as it sounds, but a good deal of time and practice *will* pay off with a strong sight vocabulary. Once a word is decoded, the child needs to use it many times and see it in different situations before it will be remembered visually. The decoding process is the initial step. But, if a word is not visually remembered in its whole form, the child will have to decode the symbols each time the word is met. This will result in slow, laborious reading.

Some children have difficulty remembering words in whole form. Usually, this is caused by lack of attention to all of the elements in the words. Many young students look only at the beginning letter and guess the rest. They simply use any word they can remember that starts with the first letter sound in the word.

There are other techniques aside from sight word knowledge that a young child can use in decoding the given word. These include picture clues and context clues.

In early reading, children are led to look at a picture and verbalize what is happening in that picture. They name the objects in pictures. They discuss the people or animals in the pictures. This type of involvement sets the stage for analyzing situations in reading.

Then, when ideas from pictures are reproduced in print, a whole new use of those pictures is introduced. If the child meets a word in sentences that cannot be decoded, he or she can refer to the picture to find an object, person, or animal that begins and ends with the same sounds. The reader is using picture clues to decide which word makes sense within the sentence.

Context clues rely on the meaning of known words where there is no picture available. The child reads all the words that he or she knows and guesses from them the meaning of the unknown word. Then an attempt is made to decode the unknown word phonetically. If this is impossible, the child will think of a word containing the same beginning and ending sounds that would make sense in that particular sentence. The new word should be studied until memorized, and used in many sentences. Usage is what makes the word a part of the child's sight vocabulary.

Words that cannot be attached to a picture but are necessary to complete meaning sometimes cause trouble in visual memory of the whole word form. They must make sense, even to the young child. Some simply must be memorized. Some words do not follow obvious phonics application. These also must be memorized so that the reader recognizes them each time they appear in print.

After phonics, picture clues, and context clues are utilized in reading, the child needs reinforcement of the words being studied. This reinforcement will increase the child's sight word recognition and strengthen his ability to comprehend what is read.

## MATERIALS TO GATHER

| | |
|---|---|
| Construction paper, assorted colors | 3″×5″ cards, unlined |
| Posterboard, assorted colors | File folders |
| Old workbooks, readers, and catalogues | Brads |
| Cardboard | Coffee filters, flat, 4″ |
| Scissors and glue | Felt-tipped pens, assorted colors |
| Shelf paper and clay | Library pockets |
| Poker chips | |

## ACTIVITIES THAT BUILD SIGHT WORD RECOGNITION

The following activities will help develop your students' sight word recognition. Be sure the concept is understood by each student.

Materials:            Manila paper, 12″ × 18″
Catalogues or workbooks
Envelopes, small
Scissors and stapler
Felt-tipped pens
Index cards, unlined
Glue

Construction:      Staple thirteen pages of manila paper together for each pupil. In the upper corners, print the alphabet letters, as shown. Cut 1″ × 3″ cards and attach a small envelope to the folder for storage. Provide workbooks or catalogues, scissors, and glue for each group of pupils.

Activity:            The pupils cut out pictures of objects that begin with the letter of each page and glue them to the appropriate sheet. You write the name of the objects on the page and make a word card for each picture. The pupils then match each word card to the picture.

**191**

Materials:        Large brown envelopes
                  Construction paper
                  Felt-tipped pens
                  Scissors

Construction:     Cut 3″ × 3″ cards from construction paper. Draw a picture
                  on each card and write the picture name on the back.
                  Square off the envelope and write a picture word in each
                  square. Store loose picture cards in the envelope.

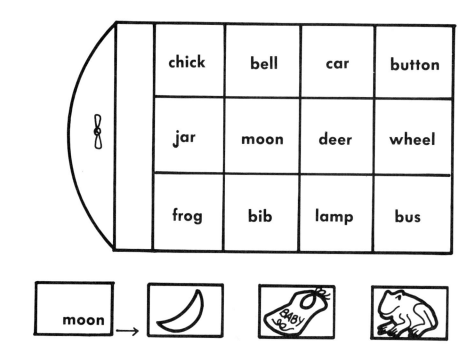

Activity:         The pupil matches each picture card to the square
                  containing the same word. The back of each picture may
                  be referred to for self-checking.

Materials:            Construction paper
                      Felt-tipped pens
                      Scissors
                      Large envelope

Construction:         Cut 3″ × 6″ cards and write a sentence on each card,
                      omitting one word. Cut out 2″ × 3″ cards. For set (a), draw
                      pictures that represent the omitted words. For set (b),
                      write only the missing words on the 2″ × 3″ cards. The
                      same sentence cards can be used for both games.

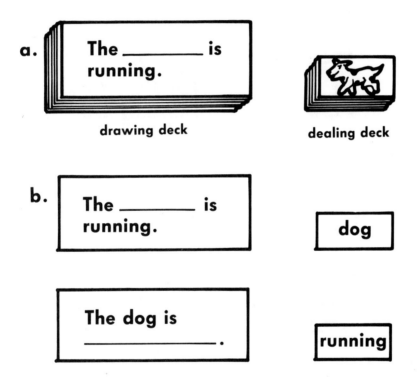

Activity:         Set a:  The sentence deck is placed on the table and
                          picture cards are dealt. A sentence card is drawn
                          and read. The pupil who has the corresponding
                          picture lays down that card.
                  Set b:  The word cards are dealt. A sentence card is
                          drawn and read. The pupil who has the correct
                          word card lays it down.

Materials:          Pictures from old workbooks
                    Posterboard and construction paper, yellow and green
                    Felt-tipped pens
                    Scissors, glue, and brads

Construction:       Make a game board as shown below. Color the alternate
                    squares yellow, white, and green. Paste a picture in the
                    yellow and green squares. On yellow and green paper,
                    write sentences that describe the pictures. Place these in
                    the pockets. Mark the spinner with numerals 1, 2, and 3
                    to determine moves.

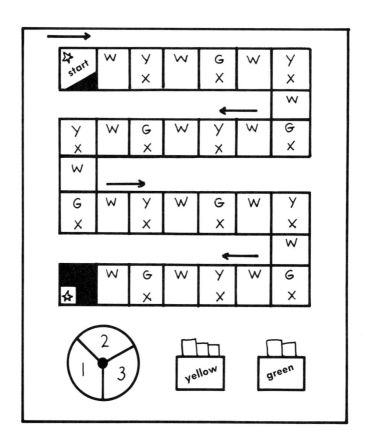

Activity:           The pupils spin and move 1, 2, or 3 steps. If the move
                    lands on a picture in the yellow or green square, a
                    sentence card is drawn from the corresponding pocket. If
                    the sentence describes the picture, the player keeps the
                    card. If not, the card is placed back into the pocket.

Materials:        Large envelopes, one per child
Index cards, unlined
Felt-tipped pens

Construction:    Make a package of word cards for each pupil. Words that can begin sentences should be written on both sides of the cards, one with a capital letter and one with a lower case letter, as shown. Make punctuation cards for each set.

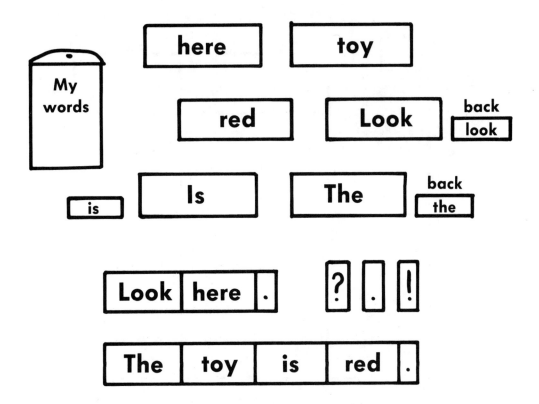

Activity:         The pupil lays all cards on the table. The teacher reads a sentence and the pupil rearranges the cards into that sentence. In this activity, word recognition, syntax, and punctuation are being reinforced.

Materials:          Index file box, 1 per child
                    Index tab cards
                    Index cards, unlined
                    Felt-tipped pens

Construction:       Supply each child with a file box and cards containing
                    capital and lower case letters on the tabs. For each pupil,
                    write word cards of words being studied.

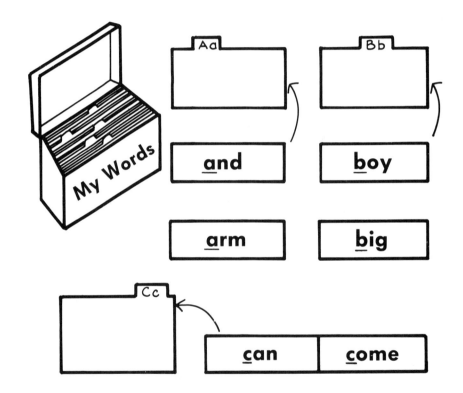

Activity:           New word cards are kept in front of the tab cards. As
                    words are learned, the pupil files each card by the first
                    letter. However, be sure to have the pupils remove the
                    filed cards and read them to you or a "buddy" periodically
                    so that they will remember the words.

Materials:              Index file box (1 per child)
                        Tagboard
                        Index tab cards, unlined
                        Felt-tipped pens
                        Scissors

Construction:           Out of tagboard, make index cards with the headings of
                        things, people, animals, doing words, color, size, and
                        question words (where, when, how). During later stages,
                        these index titles can be written on the back of the tabs:
                        nouns, verbs, adjectives, and adverbs.

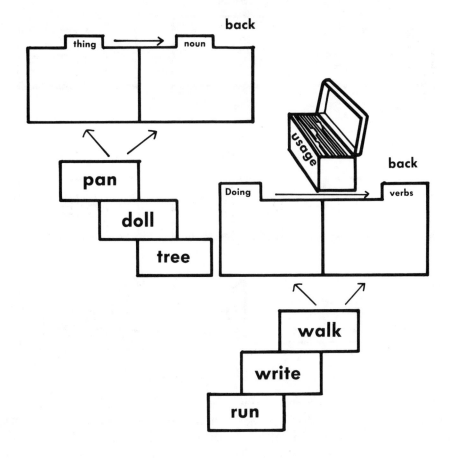

Activity:               The pupils classify words by placing their word cards
                        behind the appropriate usage heading.

Materials:          Unlined index cards
                    Felt-tipped pens
                    Brown envelopes
                    Scissors

Construction:       As shown below, write five sample cards of each word
                    being studied. Make large letters, cutting lines, and a
                    dark line across the bottom of each card. Make one model
                    card for each word. Place each set in an envelope.

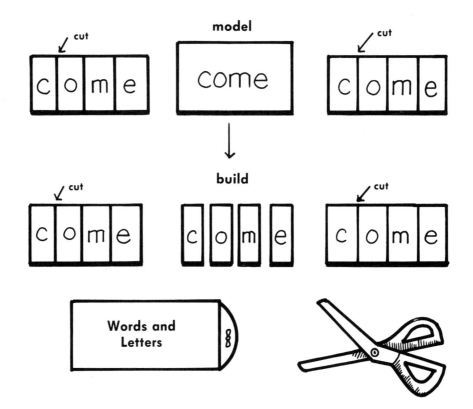

Activity:           Pupils cut the word cards on each cutting line and then,
                    rebuild the words below the model cards. This practice
                    should continue until the word is learned.

Materials:          Large macaroni
                    Word cards
                    Felt-tipped pens, fine line
                    Heavy, stiff twine

Construction:       With felt-tipped pen, write the alphabet letters on
                    macaroni. Make ten of each letter. Give each child a set of
                    lettered macaroni, twine, and word cards.

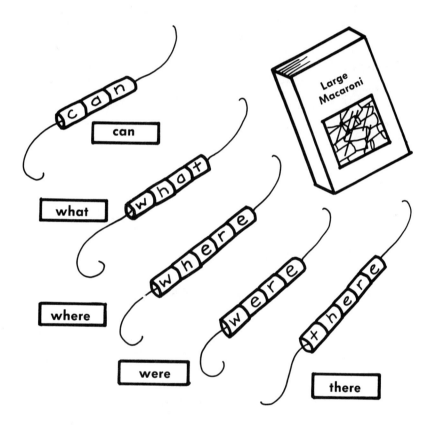

Activity:           The pupil strings the letters in proper sequence to spell
                    the words on the cards.

Materials:             Tagboard
                       Crayons, red and black
                       Scissors

Construction:          Cut $3'' \times 7''$ tagboard strips. With crayon, write words as
                       shown. The consonant letters should be written in black;
                       the vowels in red. On back of each card, write the entire
                       word in black letters.

|  |  |  | back |
|---|---|---|---|
| **some** | o, e<br>s, m | red<br>black | black<br>**some** |
| **went** | e<br>w, n, t | red<br>black | black<br>**went** |
| **want** | a<br>w, n, t | red<br>black | black<br>**want** |
| **were** | e, e<br>w, r | red<br>black | black<br>**were** |

Activity:              The pupil traces each letter with a finger and repeats the
                       word until it is memorized. The colors break the
                       elements into shorter memory units.

Name _____

Date _____

## Progress Chart

## SIGHT WORD RECOGNITION SKILLS

Not Mastered/In Progress/Mastered

| | | |
|---|---|---|
| | | |

I can match word cards to pictures.

The dog can
sit up.

Not Mastered/In Progress/Mastered

| | | |
|---|---|---|
| | | |

I can match a sentence to a picture.

The _____ is about dogs.
   (book)

Not Mastered/In Progress/Mastered

| | | |
|---|---|---|
| | | |

I can use pictures to help decode new words.

Name _____

Date _____

Progress Chart

## SIGHT WORD RECOGNITION SKILLS
### (continued)

| can | c a n |
| --- | --- |
| are | a r e |
| for | f o r |
| and | a n d |

I can build words with letter cards.

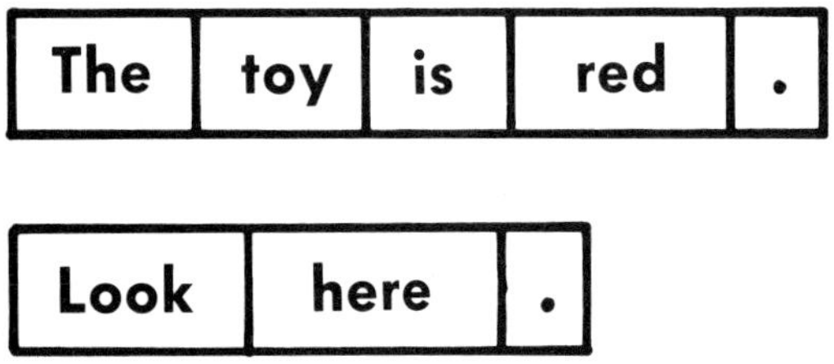

Not Mastered/In Progress/Mastered

|  |  |  |
| --- | --- | --- |

| The | toy | is | red | . |
| --- | --- | --- | --- | --- |

| Look | here | . |
| --- | --- | --- |

I can build sentences with word cards.

Not Mastered/In Progress/Mastered

|  |  |  |
| --- | --- | --- |

I can read!

Not Mastered/In Progress/Mastered

|  |  |  |
| --- | --- | --- |

Name _____

Date _____

## SIGHT WORD RECOGNITION SKILLS CHECKLIST

1. Matches word cards to appropriate pictures. _____
2. Matches sentences to appropriate pictures. _____
3. Uses pictures to help decode words in a story. _____
4. Builds words with letter cards. _____
5. Builds sentences with word cards. _____
6. Reads materials on instructional level. _____

Key:     ✔ Skill mastered
         X  Needs further instruction

## CHAPTER EIGHT

# Building Vocabulary and Comprehension Skills

Comprehension is a primary goal of reading. Does the child fully understand ideas that are put before him in print? After all of the drill for sight recognition of words, does he or she attach meaning to their uses? If not, all the other training to attain a vocabulary will be of little use to the pupil. There is more to interpretation of the text than just remembering sight words and being able to read them correctly.

## THE IMPORTANCE OF THE SKILL

The study of words in various categories helps the child understand the specific message being received from printed material. Word meanings must be studied in various settings. These settings include: antonyms (words of opposite meaning), homonyms (words of different meaning and spelling but same pronunciation), homographs (same word but different meaning), and synonyms (same meaning for different words). Others are: pronoun referents (pronouns that stand for another word or other words), words that denote what, when, where or who, including prepositional phrases, and tense (past, present, and future). It is not necessary for the child to name these categories, but their meanings must be understood. It cannot be stressed enough that oral usage should be an integral part of this training phase. The child must be involved in usage if the words are to become his or her own.

Skills that are developed in vocabulary study lead to better comprehension skills. The categories of these comprehension skills are: sequence of events, following written directions, determining a main idea, recall of facts, skimming for specific information, distinguishing facts versus fantasy or true versus false, and drawing conclusions.

Following are a list of materials and suggested activities for practice in vocabulary study. These activities include practice in word meanings, sequence, following directions, main ideas, factual recall, skimming, fact versus fantasy, and drawing conclusions.

## MATERIALS TO GATHER

File folders

Construction paper, assorted colors

Posterboard, assorted colors

Tagboard, yellow, white, and orange

Felt-tipped pens

Paper clips

Scissors

Glue

Envelopes

Index cards, unlined

Clear self-stick vinyl

Library pockets

Brads

Flat coffee filters, 4″ in diameter

Pizza boards

Book of rhymes

Tongue depressors

Clothespins

Typewriter

Shirt box

Small square box

Large brown envelopes

Rubber bands

Cardboard

Masking tape

Old readers

Children's storybooks

## ACTIVITIES THAT BUILD VOCABULARY AND COMPREHENSION SKILLS

The following activities will help develop your students' vocabulary and comprehension skills. Be sure the concepts are understood by each student.

*Word Meanings*
*(Homonyms)*

Materials:          Construction paper
                    Felt-tipped pens

Construction:       Divide the paper into eight spaces of equal size. Score
                    each side to fold back 2". On each side of the middle line
                    draw pictures that depict the words used. Write both
                    homonyms beside each picture and the answer on the
                    folded flap.

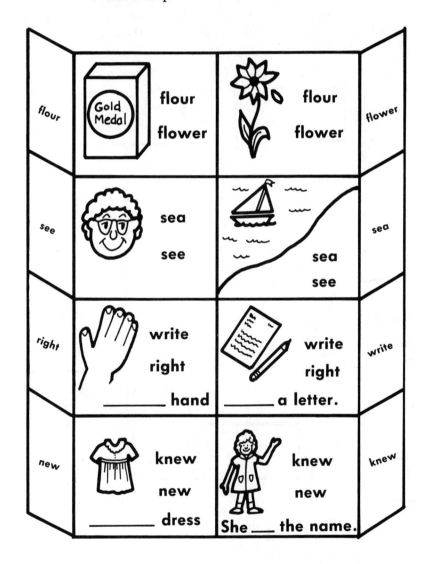

Activity:           The pupil studies the spelling and pictures of each
                    homonym. He or she then chooses the correct word. The
                    answer is on the flap for self-checking.

**207**

Materials:   Posterboard
Felt-tipped pens
Scissors
Index cards
Large brown envelope

Construction:   Cut 4″ × 2″ posterboard strips and draw a line across the middle. On each side of the line, write a word. Make a set of words that are homonyms and write the homonym pairs on an index card. Place the index card and word cards in the envelope.

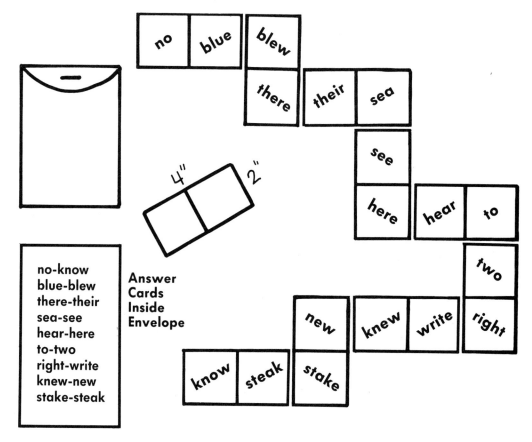

no-know
blue-blew
there-their
sea-see
hear-here
to-two
right-write
knew-new
stake-steak

**Answer
Cards
Inside
Envelope**

Activity:   The pupil pairs the homonyms by playing a domino-type game. The student can refer to the index cards for self-checking.

Materials:   File folders
        Construction paper
        Scissors
        Felt-tipped pens
        Envelope

Construction:  On a file folder, draw sailboats as shown. On one sail
        write a word. Cut separate sails out of construction
        paper. On each separate sail, write the antonym for a
        word that is written on a sailboat sail. Attach an
        envelope for storage. Write the answers on back of each
        sail.

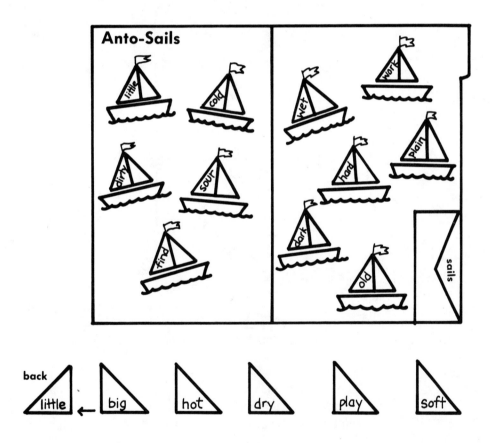

Activity:    The pupil matches each antonym sail to the word that is
        written on a sailboat sail. The student can refer to the
        back for self-checking.

Materials:
        Pizza board
        Felt-tipped pens
        Clothespins

Construction:    Divide each board, as shown. Write words on each section
and their antonyms on the back of the board. Also, write
the antonyms on clothespins. Attach these to the board in
mixed order.

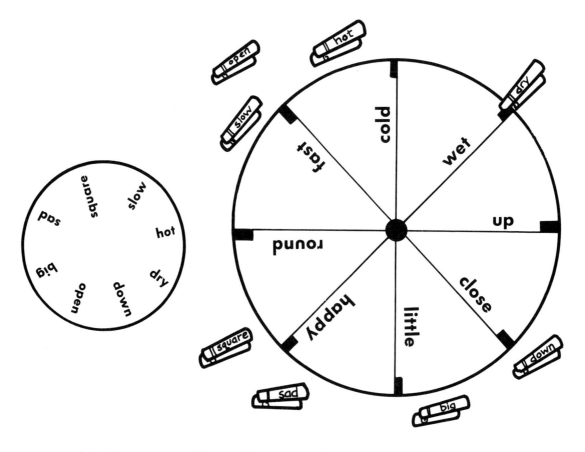

Activity:    The pupil removes the clothespins and clips each one
onto the section containing its antonym. He or she can
refer to the back of the board for the correct answer.

Materials:          Posterboard
                    Construction paper
                    Felt-tipped pens
                    Library pockets

Construction:       Draw a large Indian headdress on the posterboard. Cut
                    separate feathers out of construction paper. Write one
Style *a*           word on each headdress feather and its synonym on a
                    loose feather. Cut a slit in front of each feather in the
                    headdress. Place the loose feathers in the pocket.

Style *b*           Out of posterboard, make an Indian headdress as shown.
                    Write one word on each feather and its synonym on the
                    back.

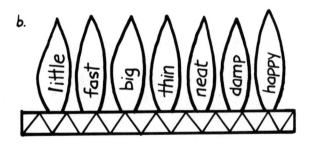

Activity:           a. Pupils match the synonym feathers to the Indian
                       headdress feathers by placing them in the appropriate
                       slits.
                    b. Pupils read the word on each feather, state its
                       synonym and look at the back to check themselves.

**211**

*Word Meanings*
*(Pronouns)*

Materials:  File folders
Felt-tipped pens
Index cards
Library pockets
Scissors
Glue

Construction:  On the left side of the folder, write two sentences in each square, one requiring a pronoun referent. On the right side of each square, write the referent. Cut index cards into $1'' \times 2''$ strips. Write the pronouns on these cards. On an index card, write the answers. Attach a pocket to hold word cards and the answer card.

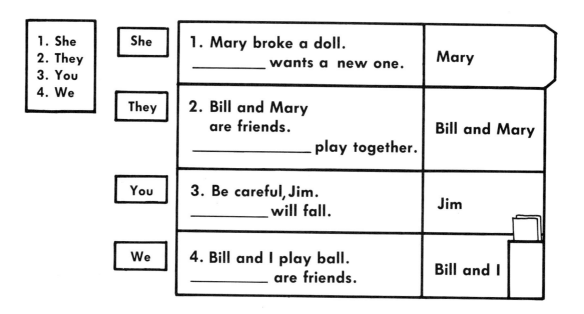

Activity:  The pupil reads each sentence and lays the appropriate pronoun card on the blank. The answer card may be referred to for self-checking.

Materials:     Large envelope
               Unlined index cards
               Felt-tipped pen
               Scissors

Construction:  On 3″ × 5″ index cards write five sentences. Underline
               the words that could be replaced by a pronoun referent.
               Cut 1″ × 5″ cards and write the pronouns on these. On
               the back of the sentence card, write the answers.

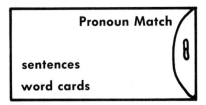

Activity:      The pupils remove the sentence and pronoun cards, then
               they read each sentence and match the pronoun referents
               to the appropriate sentence. They can check themselves
               by looking at the backs of the cards.

8-8. Words That Answer

*Word Meanings*
*(Who/Where/When/What)*

Materials:        File folders
Construction paper
Felt-tipped pens
Envelope
Scissors
Glue

Construction:    With felt-tipped pen, divide the folder and glue construction paper pockets across as shown. Write a question word on each pocket. Cut 3″ × 3″ cards and write words that denote who, what, where, and when. Write the answer on back of each card. Attach an envelope in which to store the word cards.

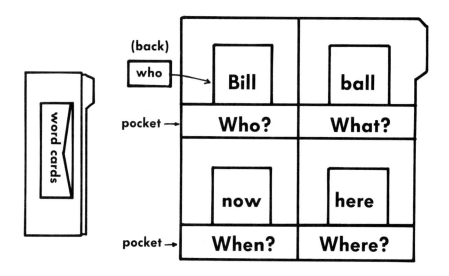

Activity:    The pupils read each word card and place each in the appropriate pocket, then refer to the back for self-checking.

214

Materials:
Pizza board
Index cards
Paperclips
Felt-tipped pens
Envelope
Scissors
Glue

Construction:
With felt-tipped pen mark off six sections. In each section write a word or a phrase that tells *where* or *when*. Cut 1″×3″ cards. On each card write the word *where* or *when*. On back, glue an envelope to hold cards and clips. Enclose an answer card for self-checking.

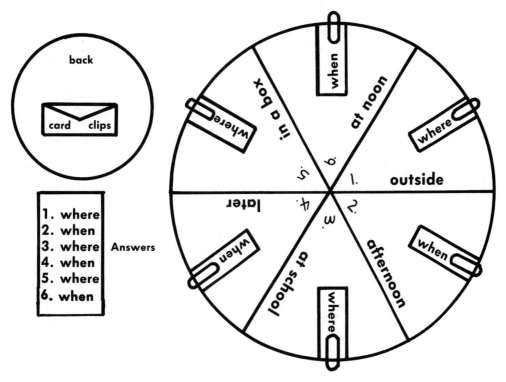

Activity:
The pupil reads the words in each section and attaches the appropriate card to signify that the words read tell *where* or *when*.

Materials:  Tongue depressors
Felt-tipped pens
Posterboard
Library pockets
Index cards, unlined
Envelope

Construction:  On index cards, draw three pictures showing stages of development. Glue each picture to a tongue depressor. On the back, write 1, 2, or 3 to signify order. On posterboard, glue three library pockets and write the numerals 1, 2, and 3. Attach an envelope to the back. Place the tongue depressors in the envelope.

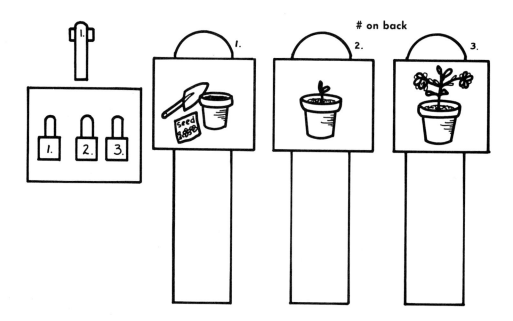

Activity:  The pupils place the tongue depressors in the pockets to signify which stage of development occurred first, next, and last. They can refer to the back for self-checking.

8-11. Square the Pictures                                    *Comprehension*
                                                             *(Sequence)*

Materials:          Construction paper
                    Old storybooks
                    Glue
                    Scissors
                    Marking pens
                    Large brown envelope

Construction:       Cut pictures from old books. Glue these to construction
                    paper and write the order numerals on the back. Draw a
                    large square on the front of the large envelope. The
                    pictures are to be placed in the envelope.

# on back

Activity:           The pupil lays out the story pictures to show the order in
                    which they occurred in the story.

8-12. Clip the Order                                    *Comprehension*
                                                        *(Sequence)*

Materials:          Pizza boards
                    Old storybooks
                    Scissors
                    Clothespins
                    Felt-tipped pens
                    Glue

Construction:       Divide the pizza board into four sections. Cut pictures
                    from a familiar story and glue these, out of sequence, to
                    the pizza board. On clothespins write the numerals 1, 2,
                    3, and 4. On the back of each picture, write the correct
                    sequence numeral.

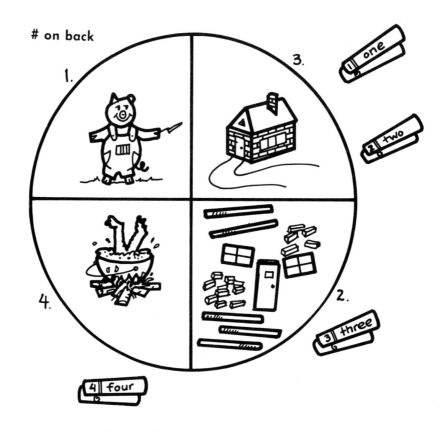

Activity:           The pupil clips the numeral pins beside each picture to
                    denote the sequence of events and then refers to the back
                    for self-checking.

218

Materials:      Construction paper, 9″ × 12″
Storybook
Envelope
Scissors
Index cards
Glue
Felt-tipped pens

Construction:      Cut out one paragraph from a story and glue it to the construction paper. Below this, draw lines and number them. Write sentence strips from the story and place the order number on the back of each card. Glue an envelope to the back to hold the sentence strips.

**back**

**sentences**

One day the rains came. Mother duck went to the shore. Two little brown ducklings followed. The white duckling stayed behind.

Place sentence strips in order.

1   The rains came. _____
2 _____
3 _____
4 _____

Activity:      The pupil reads the paragraph and the sentence strips. Then, he or she places the sentences in correct sequence. The back of each card may be referred to for self-checking.

*Comprehension*
*(Following Directions)*

Materials:     One small box
               Index cards, unlined
               Scissors
               Felt-tipped pens
               Construction paper
               Glue

Construction:  Cover the box with construction paper and draw a large
               question mark on the front. Cut index cards into $3'' \times 5''$
               strips. Write single sentence directions on each strip and
               fold it over twice. Make some directions humorous. Use
               words the children know or are learning to recognize.
               Place the cards into the box.

**Look at a book.**

**Paint a picture.**

Activity:      Each pupil draws one sentence strip, reads the directions,
               and acts them out. No oral communication takes place.
               The class is to guess what the directions stated.

Materials:          Large box with low sides
Crayons
Glue
Paper
Pencil
Index cards
Scissors
Felt-tipped pens
Library pockets

Construction:      On index cards write 15 activities. On each set of 5 cards, write numerals 1, 2, and 3. Glue three library pockets to the box lid and on these write the numerals 1, 2, and 3. Place the cards in the corresponding pockets. The activities should all be equally difficult.

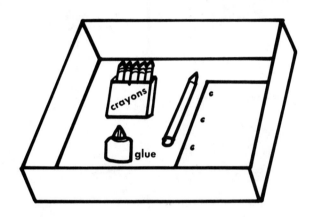

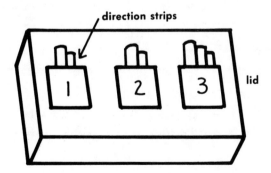

Activity:          The pupils must do one activity from each pocket in order (1, 2, and 3) before going back to the first pocket. This simply adds an element of surprise and expectation.

**221**

*Comprehension*
*(Following Directions)*

Materials: Posterboard
Felt-tipped pens

Construction: For less independent pupils, this chart of station assignments can be made. Divide the posterboard into 4 sections and draw a picture of each type of activity that pupils can do, in a particular order. The first activity may be to read or look at a book; second, to paint; third, to write; and, fourth, to use the listening station.

Activity: The pupils will follow the activity schedule by doing the activities that are depicted, in the same order as shown.

8-17. Go Fish *Comprehension (Following Directions)*

Materials: Posterboard
Library pockets, 1 per child
Net bag
Felt-tipped pens
Construction paper
Scissors
Glue

Construction: Paste pockets with pupils' names on them in rows on the posterboard. Cut 1″ × 5″ strips of construction paper and attach a pocket to hold these strips. Cut fish out of construction paper and write an activity on each fish. Attach a net to hold the fish.

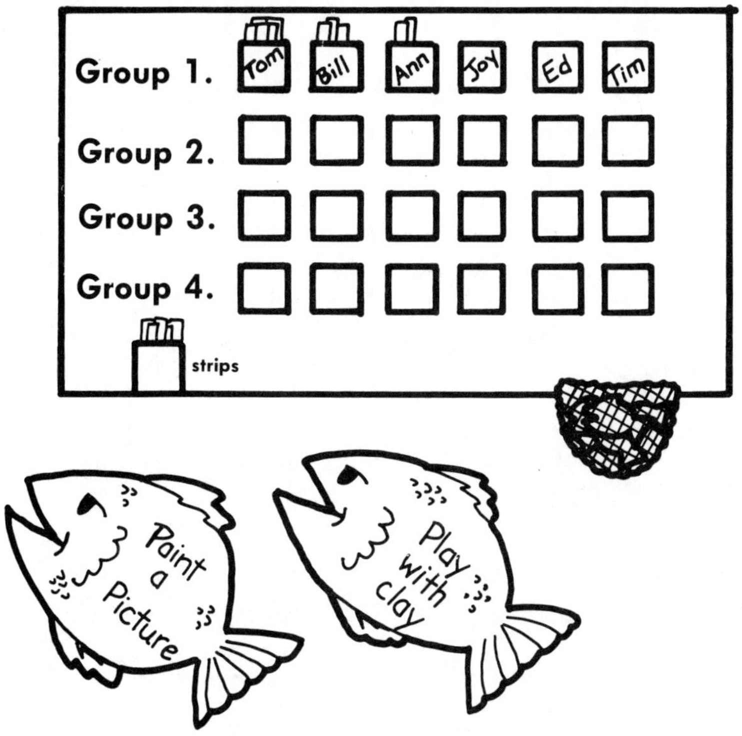

Activity: As you notice a pupil doing something well, remaining on task, or completing an assignment, place a strip in his or her pocket. Each strip is worth 5 points. When the pupil collects 3 strips, he or she may draw a fish from the net and do a special activity.

Materials:        Tagboard
Typewriter
Envelopes
Scissors

Construction:        Using the pattern below, cut hexagonal shapes out of tagboard. Type or print a short paragraph and the question, "What is the *Main Idea?*" on the top half. On the bottom half, type or print the main idea of the paragraph. Cut between the question and the main idea. Place the pieces in an envelope.

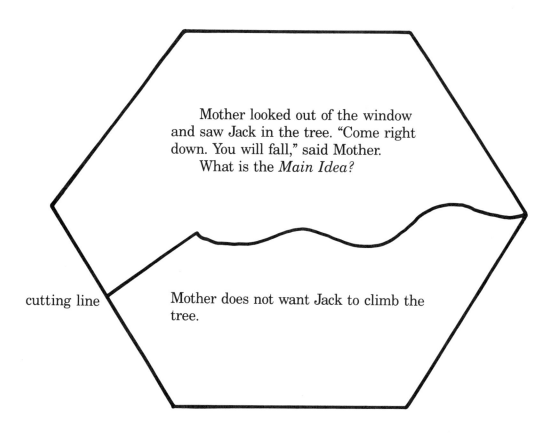

Mother looked out of the window and saw Jack in the tree. "Come right down. You will fall," said Mother. What is the *Main Idea?*

cutting line

Mother does not want Jack to climb the tree.

Activity:        The pupil matches the main idea to the appropriate paragraph by completing each puzzle.

Materials:          Posterboard, $8'' \times 11''$
                         Construction paper
                         Clear self-stick vinyl
                         Typewriter or felt-tipped pen
                         Scissors
                         Glue

Construction:    Cut construction paper strips, $6'' \times 3\frac{1}{2}''$, and fold each in half. On the front side, type a paragraph or short story. Inside, type or write three choices of titles. Write the answer verso the story, as shown. Glue the back of the title portion to posterboard. Cover the titles with clear self-stick vinyl.

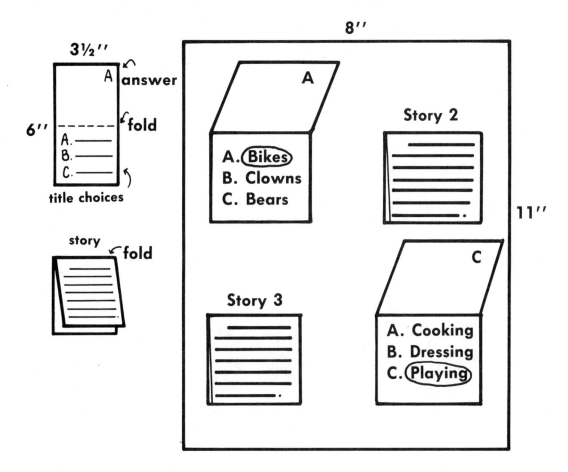

Activity:          The pupil reads each story and circles the title. The answers may be checked by looking on the story flap.

8-20. Main Idea Kites                                          *Main Idea*

Materials:        File folder
                  Construction paper
                  Scissors
                  Typewriter
                  Felt-tipped pens
                  Library pockets
                  Glue

Construction:     Using the pattern below, cut kites and tails out of
                  construction paper. On each kite, type a short story or
                  paragraph and the question, "What is the *Main Idea?*"
                  On each tail, type a main idea on the front and the story
                  number on the back. Glue the kites to a folder, number
                  each story, and draw strings and tails. Attach a pocket to
                  hold the loose tails.

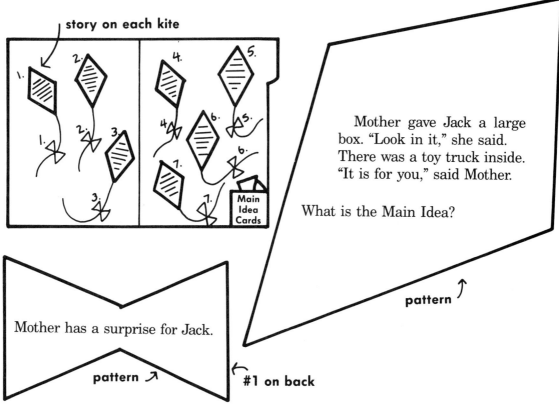

**story on each kite**

Mother gave Jack a large box. "Look in it," she said. There was a toy truck inside. "It is for you," said Mother.

What is the Main Idea?

**pattern** ↑

Mother has a surprise for Jack.

**pattern** ↗

← **#1 on back**

Activity:         The pupil reads each kite paragraph and matches the
                  appropriate main idea tail. He or she may refer to the
                  back of each tail for self-checking.

Materials:            File folder
                      Construction paper
                      Typewriter
                      Felt-tipped pens
                      Library pockets
                      Scissors
                      Glue

Construction:         Using the pattern below, cut out six construction paper
                      balloons and type a story and number on each one. Trace
                      six balloons on the folder, draw strings, and write a main
                      idea and number to match the stories. Attach a pocket to
                      hold the loose balloons.

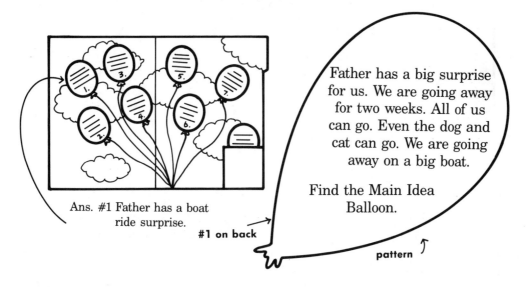

Ans. #1 Father has a boat
ride surprise.
#1 on back

Father has a big surprise
for us. We are going away
for two weeks. All of us
can go. Even the dog and
cat can go. We are going
away on a big boat.

Find the Main Idea
Balloon.

pattern ʔ

Activity:             The child reads the balloon stories and matches each one
                      to the correct main idea balloon. The numbers on back
                      may be referred to for self-checking.

Materials:    Large brown envelopes
              Library pockets
              Basal reading textbooks
              Typewriter
              Index cards

Construction: Fold the library pocket down to form a flap over the
              pocket. Type a paragraph from the reader and label it
              with the reading level, unit, and story source. On an
              index card, type factual questions on the front and
              answers on the back. Label cards and envelopes with the
              reading level and story source. Place the question cards
              in pockets and the pockets in envelopes.

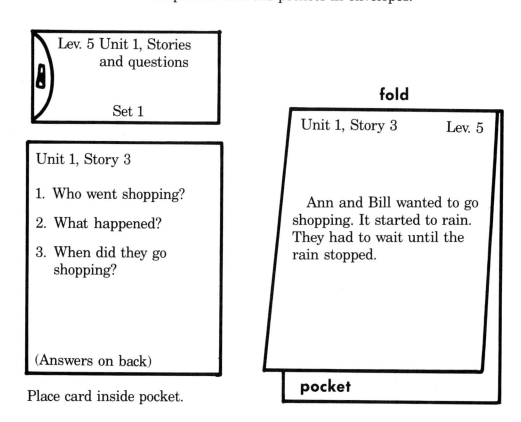

Lev. 5 Unit 1, Stories
and questions

Set 1

**fold**

Unit 1, Story 3        Lev. 5

Ann and Bill wanted to go
shopping. It started to rain.
They had to wait until the
rain stopped.

**pocket**

Unit 1, Story 3

1. Who went shopping?

2. What happened?

3. When did they go
   shopping?

(Answers on back)

Place card inside pocket.

Activity:     The pupil reads the story on each pocket and answers
              the questions on the card inside. He or she may refer to
              the back for self-checking.

**228**

| | |
|---|---|
| Materials: | Posterboard, 8″ × 10″<br>Construction paper<br>Scissors<br>Typewriter<br>Razor blade, single-edged<br>Envelope<br>Glue |
| Construction: | Cut 4″ × 6″ construction paper cards and type a rhyme on each card. Glue these to the posterboard. On the bottom half, type questions about each rhyme. To the right of each question, cut a slit as shown. On small answer cards, type the exact words from context that answer each question. Write the question number on back and attach an envelope to store the cards. |

| | |
|---|---|
| Activity: | The pupil reads the rhyme and question cards. Then, he or she places each answer card in the slit beside the appropriate question. The back of each card may be referred to for self-checking. |

Materials:    Posterboard, $8'' \times 10''$
Library pockets
Scissors
Glue
Felt-tipped pens
Index cards

Construction:    Using the pattern below, cut kites out of construction paper. On each kite write a short story and attach it to the posterboard. Draw the tails and attach a pocket beneath the kite and story. Write questions on an index card and place it in the pocket. Make answer tails, number each one for self-checking, and place these in the answer pocket.

Activity:    The pupil reads the story and question card. Then, the answer tails are removed and placed on the corresponding question tails on the posterboard. Students may refer to the back for self-checking.

## Skimming for Information

Being able to find specific information in a hurry will be a valuable tool for each child in higher grades. The idea of skimming lines of print to find information can be started early in group directed lessons. If students are readied for this skill in first and second grades, they will develop the concept more easily in intermediate grades.

Show the pupils how to sweep across a line of print with a pencil or finger. They should read only the word or words in question, and merely glance at the other words without concentrating on them for visual recognition.

1. Have the pupils find a specific word being studied on a page of print. You read the page first to find how many times that particular word appears. Then tell the student, "Underline the word *and* everytime you see it on this page." If you know there were eight and the pupil found only six, tell him to find two more.

2. Copy a page, leaving key words blank. Put the beginning letter on the blank. Tell the pupils the page number and have them locate each missing word and write it on the line. Example:
   The d_____ is brown and wh_____. (page 17) (dog and white)

3. Number the lines on a page from an old storybook. Select five lines to write on a piece of paper, leaving one word out of each line. On the blank, place the page number and line number (no letter). The pupils locate the correct line and write the missing word. Example: Jane went to the p. 13, L. 6 with Dad. (farm)

4. If a particular phonic element is being studied, have the pupils skim to locate words containing that element. Example: "On this page find five words beginning with *sh*."

5. From a specific page, have the pupils locate words that are names, toy, or animals.

## Fact versus Fantasy or True versus False

When nursery rhymes and stories are being read to children, it is good to establish the idea of "make-believe." While developing an active imagination is healthy, the child needs to be able to distinguish between what is true and what is make-believe.

1. Cut pictures from different types of children's books. Paste these to a folder and, beside each picture, draw a person and an elf. If the action in the picture is possible, the child points to the person. If the action is impossible, the child points to the elf.

2. Give each child a card with the words "yes" and "no" written on alternate sides. You read short excerpts from stories. The pupils hold up a "yes" response if the story action is possible; and "no" response if the action is impossible.

3. Variation of 2: The child uses the faces to label riddles as true or false.

4. Divide the bottom of a shallow box, and draw a happy face and a sad face. Let the pupils cut out pictures from old workbooks. These pictures are to be placed on the correct side of the box depicting true (happy face) or false (sad face). Any logical explanations the students offer should be accepted.

5. Advertisements sometimes show animated articles such as a talking tooth or a piece of fruit. Include these in the collection for the child to separate and distinguish.

6. Verbalize facts and non-truths with the pupils. Give examples and ask pupils to shake or nod their heads in response to your statements. Then, let the pupils give some examples.

7. When the pupils can read the words *yes* and *no,* have them separate pictures into envelopes on which these words are written.

## Drawing Conclusions

The ability to determine what will probably happen based on what has already happened depends on experiences within the child's background. The child who has been exposed to the verbal exchange of ideas throughout the preschool years will not find this difficult. However, basic readiness for this higher skill can begin to develop in early primary grades. Remember! Every higher skill must be built on a foundation of readiness preparation.

1. *What If?* Make up short unfinished stories and ask the pupils what would happen. Example: "What if Jane went outside in the rain?" (She would get wet.) "What if you went to school with only one shoe?" Use ideas the pupils understand. Accept their words. Don't expect specific wording based on how you would answer.

2. Use pictures from nursery rhymes or children's books. Show the pupils a picture of "Jack falling down the hill." Ask them how Jack would feel after that fall. "What happened to the water?"

3. Use the classroom sink and a cup. Fill a cup with water and show this to the pupils. Pour some water out and ask the class why there is a lesser amount. You want them to realize that the new volume is the conclusion of an action.

4. Have students mix dough in class. Let them taste the mixture at different stages. They should come to the conclusion that as each ingredient is added, the taste changes.

5. *Tell Me Why:* Use pictures of actions or make verbal statements about actions. Example:

   Show the picture of a wet duck. Let the child explain why the duck is wet. Accept any possible answer.

   Verbal: Say "The house burned down." Let a child give his or her idea of what may have happened.

Name —————————————————————

Date —————————————————————

## Progress Chart

## VOCABULARY and COMPREHENSION SKILLS

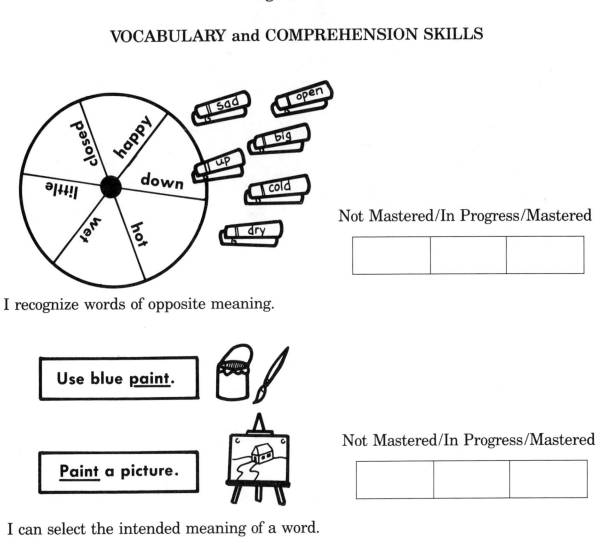

Not Mastered/In Progress/Mastered

| | | |
|---|---|---|
| | | |

I recognize words of opposite meaning.

Use blue <u>paint</u>.

<u>Paint</u> a picture.

Not Mastered/In Progress/Mastered

| | | |
|---|---|---|
| | | |

I can select the intended meaning of a word.

Not Mastered/In Progress/Mastered

| | | |
|---|---|---|
| | | |

I can match two words that mean the same.

Name _____

Date _____

Progress Chart

## VOCABULARY and COMPREHENSION SKILLS
### (continued)

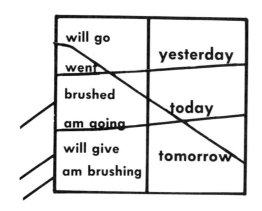

Not Mastered/In Progress/Mastered

| | | |
|---|---|---|
| | | |

I can select words that denote yesterday, today, and tomorrow in meaning.

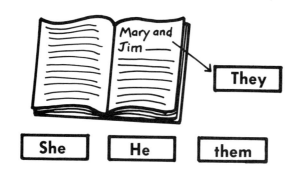

Not Mastered/In Progress/Mastered

| | | |
|---|---|---|
| | | |

I can locate the word a pronoun represents.

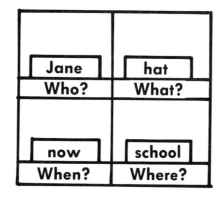

Not Mastered/In Progress/Mastered

| | | |
|---|---|---|
| | | |

I recognize words that tell what, when, where, and who.

Name _____

Date _____

**Progress Chart**

**VOCABULARY and COMPREHENSION SKILLS**
(continued)

**COMPREHENSION**

Not Mastered/In Progress/Mastered

| | | |
|---|---|---|
| | | |

I can recognize what happens first, second, and last.

Not Mastered/In Progress/Mastered

| | | |
|---|---|---|
| | | |

I can follow oral and written directions.

Not Mastered/In Progress/Mastered

| | | |
|---|---|---|
| | | |

I can give a story or a picture a name.

Name _____

Date _____

**Progress Chart**

**VOCABULARY and COMPREHENSION SKILLS**
(continued)

I can remember what I read and heard.

Not Mastered/In Progress/Mastered

| | | |
|---|---|---|
| | | |

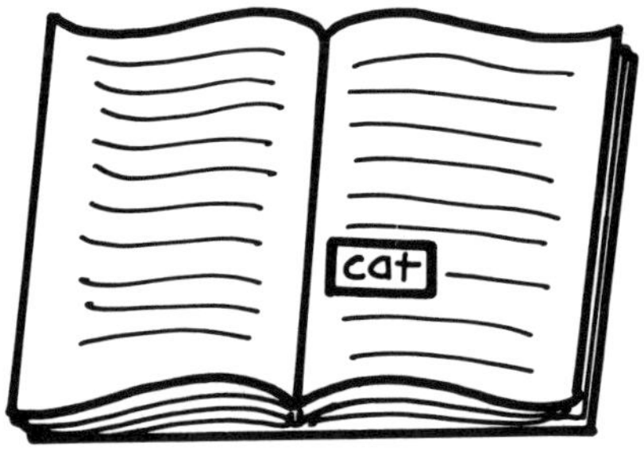

I can find specific words on a page.

Not Mastered/In Progress/Mastered

| | | |
|---|---|---|
| | | |

I can distinguish fact from fantasy.

Not Mastered/In Progress/Mastered

| | | |
|---|---|---|
| | | |

Name _____

Date _____

## Progress Chart

## VOCABULARY and COMPREHENSION SKILLS
### (continued)

"I will get wet."

Not Mastered/In Progress/Mastered

|  |  |  |
|---|---|---|
|  |  |  |

I know what will happen if... I walk in the rain.
    (Drawing Conclusions)

Name _____

Date _____

# VOCABULARY and COMPREHENSION SKILLS CHECKLIST

## VOCABULARY WORD MEANINGS

1. Recognizes words of opposite meaning (antonyms). _____
2. Selects the intended meaning of a word (homographs). _____
3. Selects two words that mean the same (synonyms). _____
4. Correctly uses tense. _____
5. Correctly uses pronoun referents. _____
6. Recognizes words that tell what, when, who and where. _____

## COMPREHENSION

1. Recalls correct story sequence. _____
2. Follows oral and written directions. _____
3. Distinguishes the main idea. _____
4. Recalls facts. _____
5. Locates specific words on a page. _____
6. Distinguishes real and make-believe. _____
7. Draws conclusions based on past experiences.

| Key: | ✔ Skill mastered |
|---|---|
| | X Needs further instruction |

© 1987 by The Center for Applied Research in Education

# Appendix A

## GLOSSARY OF READING TERMS

ANTONYMS: Words representing opposite meanings of one another.

AUDITORY ACUITY: Sharpness of hearing. How clearly sounds are heard and distinguished.

AUDITORY DISCRIMINATION: The ability to distinguish likenesses and differences between two or more sounds.

AUDITORY FIGURE-GROUND: The ability to keep one's attention on specific sounds while ignoring surrounding sounds within the background.

AUDITORY MEMORY: The ability to store information mentally and to remember what one has heard over a period of time.

AUDITORY PERCEPTION: The ability to interpret and discriminate incoming sounds.

AUDITORY SEQUENCING: The ability to remember the order of items or information that is heard.

AUDITORY SOUND-BLENDING: The ability to remember and blend letter sounds in correct sequence when decoding words.

BODY AWARENESS: Knowledge of the body itself. It consists of three elements; body image, concept, and schema, in that order of development.

BODY CONCEPT: Intellectual knowledge of one's body; that it is separate and away from other visual stimuli, and that it consists of two arms and legs, one head, two eyes, one nose and mouth, and so forth.

BODY SCHEMA: Unconscious idea of body movement. The legs and arms move forward and back when mobilizing oneself without consciously thinking the actions.

COMPOUNDS: Words containing two complete words. (raincoat)

COMPREHENSION: Interpretation of printed symbols by attaching meaning to these symbols and understanding the author's intent.

CONSONANT BLENDS: Two consonant letters written together, each letter sound being pronounced. (*fl*ag)

CONSONANT DIGRAPHS: Two consonants written together but exhibiting one different sound (not the regular sound of either consonant).

CONSONANT LETTERS: All letters of the alphabet with the exceptions of a, e, i, o, and u. Most of these letters represent only one distinct sound.

CONTEXT: The written or oral material in which a word is used. The sentence or paragraph that contains the word or words in question.

CONTRACTION: A combination of two words made by omitting one or more letters and inserting an apostrophe. (can not . . . can't)

DIRECTIONALITY: Knowledge of left and right in space. Ability to look away from one's body and determine the left and right sides of another object.

FIGURE-GROUND PERCEPTION: The ability to focus attention on one main object, ignoring other surrounding objects within the visual field.

HOMOGRAPHS: The same word but different meanings dependent upon context and usage.

HOMONYMS: Words of different meaning and spelling, but the same pronunciation.

INTELLIGENCE: An inherited trait of potential to learn.

LATERALITY: Knowledge of the left and right sides of the body.

MATURATION: An orderly and sequential nervous system development.

MENTAL AGE: The level of a child's development at a given time.

PERCEPTUAL CONSTANCY: Ability to recognize an object as having constant characteristics regardless of its angle or how it is shown.

PHONETIC SPELLING PATTERNS: The visual sequence of letters exhibiting consistent sound blending that determines pronunciation of words.

PHONICS: The study of letter sounds.

POSITION-IN-SPACE PERCEPTION: The interpretation of the relationship of an object to the observer. Where, looking away from the body, is an object that is seen?

PRONOUNS: Words that stand for other words as objects or persons.

SPATIAL RELATIONSHIP PERCEPTION: The ability to relate position of two or more objects to oneself and to each other.

STRUCTURAL ANALYSIS: The study of specific word parts, such as endings, prefixes, and suffixes. Also included are compound words and contractions.

SYLLABLES: Separate pronounced parts within a word.

SYMBOL/SOUND RELATIONSHIP: The association of a letter or letters to a particular sound.

SYNONYMS: Two different words that have the same meaning.

TENSE: Words that denote time in the past, present, or future.

UTILITY WORDS: Words that cannot be visualized but are necessary to combine other words into meaningful units as sentences; such as: of, the, to, for, and the like.

VISUAL ACUITY: Sharpness of vision. How clearly is an object or word seen?

VISUAL-MOTOR: The ability to coordinate vision with movements of the body.

VISUAL PERCEPTION: The interpretation of what one sees.

VOWELS: The letters a, e, i, o, u, and sometimes y and w. Each vowel represents two or more sounds.

VOWEL DIGRAPHS: Combinations of two vowels that represent only one vowel sound. (oa, ai, ee)

VOWEL DIPHTHONGS: Combinations of two vowels that exhibit a third and different sound when written together. (ou, oo, oy)

WORD ENDINGS: Additional letters at the end of a word; such as, *s, ed, ing,* or *ly.*

WORD RECOGNITION VOCABULARY: Words that a student recognizes instantly on sight, in any context.

# Appendix B

## SAMPLE WORD LISTS

### 1. Consonant Blends and Digraphs

*"L" Blends*

| bl | cl | fl | gl | pl | sl |
|---|---|---|---|---|---|
| blanket | clock | flag | glove | play | sleep |
| block | clown | flow | glare | plus | slap |
| bleak | claw | flower | glow | please | slip |
| blind | clay | flit | gleam | plow | slope |
| blue | clear | flute | glad | plaid | slim |
| blow | close | fly | glitter | plank | slink |

*"R" Blends*

| br | cr | dr | fr | gr | pr | tr |
|---|---|---|---|---|---|---|
| brown | crow | dress | frog | grass | pray | |
| break | crown | draw | fresh | green | prowl | |
| brick | crack | dream | frisky | great | prince | |
| brow | crook | drag | frank | gross | prance | |
| brook | crank | drink | frill | grew | pretzel | |
| brain | crimp | drank | fright | growl | proud | |

*"S" Blends*

| sc/sk | sm | sn | sp | st/str | sw |
|---|---|---|---|---|---|
| scale | smile | snake | spill | stink | swing |
| skate | small | snow | spank | stall | swim |
| scrub | smell | snatch | spar | stalk | swam |
| scat | smart | sniff | spring | start | swat |
| skin | smog | snap | spider | stake | sweep |
| skill | smear | snarl | spike | string | sweet |
| skim | smoke | snag | spice | street | swift |
| skin | smite | snip | spell | stride | switch |

*Digraphs*

| ch | sh | th | wh |
|---|---|---|---|
| chain | she | the | whale |

| cherry | show | they | while |
| chip | shower | them | whine |
| chipmunk | ship | this | where |
| chant | shall | that | what |
| child | shovel | thank | whelp |
| chicken | shot | thaw | which |

## 2. Word Families

| *at* | *an* | *ay* | *ar* | *and* | *ake* |
|------|------|------|------|-------|-------|
| bat | ban | bay | bar | band | bake |
| cat | can | day | car | hand | cake |
| fat | Dan | hay | far | land | fake |
| hat | fan | jay | jar | sand | lake |
| mat | man | may | mar | stand | make |
| pat | pan | pay | par | | rake |
| rat | ran | play | star | | take |
| sat | tan | stay | tar | | wake |

| *ame* | *ade* | *ed* | *en* | *et* | *ell* |
|-------|-------|------|------|------|-------|
| came | bade | bed | Ben | bet | bell |
| dame | fade | fed | den | get | cell |
| fame | jade | led | hen | jet | fell |
| frame | shade | Ned | Ken | let | sell |
| same | trade | red | men | pet | tell |

| *est* | *ig* | *in* | *it* | *ip* | *ick* |
|-------|------|------|------|------|-------|
| best | big | bin | bit | dip | Dick |
| nest | dig | fin | fit | drip | kick |
| pest | fig | gin | hit | hip | lick |
| rest | pig | kin | lit | rip | Nick |
| test | wig | pin | mit | sip | sick |
| vest | rig | win | sit | whip | tick |

| *ill* | *ist* | *ike* | *ind* | *og* | *op* |
|-------|-------|-------|-------|------|------|
| bill | fist | bike | bind | bog | bop |
| dill | list | dike | find | cog | cop |
| fill | mist | hike | hind | dog | hop |
| gill | twist | Mike | kind | fog | mop |
| hill | wrist | tike | mind | frog | pop |
| Jill | | yike | rind | log | stop |
| mill | | | | | |

| *ook* | *oon* | *ock* | *ug* | *un* | *ump* |
|-------|-------|-------|------|------|-------|
| book | boon | block | bug | bun | bump |
| cook | coon | clock | dug | fun | dump |

| hook | goon  | cock  | hug | gun  | hump |
|------|-------|-------|-----|------|------|
| look | moon  | dock  | jug | run  | jump |
| nook | noon  | lock  | mug | sun  | lump |
| rook | spoon | stock | rug | stun | mump |

## 3. Phonetic Patterns and Vowel Spelling Combinations

### CVC (Short Vowels)

| ă | ĕ | ĭ | ŏ | ŭ |
|------|-----|-----|-----|-----|
| man | pet | him | Bob | bug |
| had | bed | hit | got | put |
| trap | let | sit | lot | hut |
| ham | hen | pin | log | cup |
| cap | pen | lid | not | fun |
| pan | yes | did | fox | mud |

### CVCė (Long Vowels)

| ā-ė | ī-ė | ō-ė | ū-ė |
|------|------|------|------|
| bake | dime | rope | cute |
| gate | kite | nose | mule |
| face | pipe | hose | cube |
| cave | mine | mope | fuse |
| game | like | rose | mute |

### CVƀ C (Long Vowels)

| āł | ēȧ | ēė | īė | ōȧ |
|-------|-------|--------|-----|------|
| tail | bead | see | pie | boat |
| paid | read | jeep | tie | coat |
| rain | team | seed | lie | goat |
| maid | weak | beet | die | load |
| rail | lead | tree | | road |
| paint | reach | street | | toad |
| chain | seat | deer | | roam |

### Vowel Diphthongs

| aw | au | o̅o̅ | ŏu | ou |
|-------|-------|-------|-------|--------|
| caw | haul | boon | book | cloud |
| saw | haunt | boot | cook | loud |
| bawl | maul | root | look | sound |
| crawl | taut | moon | hook | round |
| lawn | cause | roost | took | out |
| jaw | pause | spoon | crook | spout |
| drawn | fault | broom | brook | ground |

| ow | oi | oy |
|---|---|---|
| cow | coil | boy |
| owl | boil | toy |
| now | voice | joy |
| fowl | spoil | enjoy |
| brow | foil | Roy |
| crown | choice | coy |
| clown | point | Roy |
| vowel | coin | soy |

*Vowel "R" Control*

| er | ir | ur |
|---|---|---|
| her | fir | fur |
| herd | first | purr |
| pert | skirt | burst |
| fern | bird | purse |
| perch | stir | burn |
| herb | girl | curl |
| verse | shirt | churn |
| jerk | thirst | nurse |

## 4. Affixes: Prefixes, Suffixes, Contractions, and Compounds

*Prefixes*

| dis | re | un |
|---|---|---|
| disagree | rewrite | undress |
| discolor | redo | unlock |
| disconnect | reread | undo |
| dishonest | refold | unhappy |
| dislike | repay | unclean |
| disobey | recolor | untie |
| displeased | reload | unopened |
| distrust | rewrap | unfair |

*Suffixes*

| er | ly | ful |
|---|---|---|
| brighter | slowly | playful |
| longer | gladly | helpful |
| harder | loudly | cheerful |
| slower | nicely | useful |
| funnier | happily | hopeful |
| happier | sadly | painful |
| colder | sweetly | harmful |
| faster | quickly | joyful |

*Contractions*

| | | |
|---|---|---|
| didn't | aren't | can't |
| doesn't | hasn't | couldn't |
| haven't | won't | don't |
| I'm | I'll | we're |
| I've | it's | wasn't |
| we've | they'll | he'll |
| isn't | weren't | we'll |
| there's | let's | he's |
| she's | that's | you've |
| she'll | you'll | I'd |

*Compounds*

| | | |
|---|---|---|
| dustpan | mailman | starfish |
| wishbone | rosebud | windmill |
| farmyard | rowboat | backbone |
| cookbook | paintbrush | playmate |
| sunshine | drumstick | raincoat |
| pancakes | handbag | bathtub |
| toothbrush | milkman | rainbow |
| sandman | placemat | sunset |
| snowman | popcorn | raindrop |

## 5. Antonyms, Homonyms, and Synonyms

*Antonyms*

| | |
|---|---|
| night-day | hot-cold |
| up-down | in-out |
| far-near | heavy-light |
| create-destroy | full-empty |
| big-little | push-pull |
| open-close | front-back |
| same-different | dry-wet |
| rough-smooth | work-play |
| hard-soft | plain-fancy |
| sweet-sour | dirty-clean |
| lose-find | dark-light |
| old-new | wild-tame |
| safe-dangerous | deep-shallow |
| weak-strong | over-under |

*Homonyms*

| | |
|---|---|
| bear-bare | flee-flea |
| herd-heard | hare-hair |
| son-sun | cent-sent |

flower-flour          peak-peek
pain-pane             tale-tail
rap-wrap              ring-wring
chili-chilly          stake-steak
board-bored           whale-wail
raise-rays            wait-weight
whole-hole            sell-cell
horse-hoarse          toe-tow
steel-steal           rain-rein

*Synonyms*

loud-noisy            sick-ill
angry-mad             thin-skinny
empty-hollow          friend-playmate
damp-wet              catch-capture
laugh-giggle          bug-insect
gift-present          find-discover
baby-infant           ache-pain
scared-frightened     copy-imitate
order-command         shout-yell
happy-glad            cry-weep

# Appendix C

## SOURCES FOR REFERRALS AND SKILLS TESTS

*County School Board of Public Instruction* Referrals:

*County School Board Psychological Services* for testing of:
      learning potential
      specific learning disability
      visual screening
*County School Board Speech and Hearing Division* for
testing of: speech evaluation
           hearing evaluation

### Commercial Criterion Reference Skills Tests

Criterion reference tests give precise evaluative information that aids the teacher in individualizing instruction for each pupil. The tests mentioned here are diagnostic in that they pinpoint strengths and weaknesses of each reading skill. Also, each one is quick and easy to administer and can be given to an entire class.

*Fountain Valley Teacher Support System in Reading*
      Red Level.... 1.0
      Orange Level.... 2.0
      from: Richard L. Zweig Associates, Inc.
           20800 Beach Blvd.
           Huntington Beach, Calif., 92648
*Prescriptive Reading Inventory*
      Level Red/A.... Grades 1.5–2.5
      Level Green/B.... Grades 2.0–3.5
      from: CTB/McGraw-Hill
           Manchester Road
           Manchester, Mo., 63011

*Commercial Oral Reading Inventory* to test the level of skill application, and to provide diagnostic information that relates directly to instructional decision making.

*Progressive Reading Evaluation Portfolio* which consists of three diagnostic devices: the Joels-Anderson-Thompson (JAT) Reading Inventory, the Prereading Skills Assessment, and the Primary Reading Skills Assessment. This battery yields information such as:

> independent, instructional, and frustration levels
>
> oral miscues
>
> auditory discrimination
>
> letter recognition
>
> oral cloze
>
> word recognition and vocabulary
>
> word attack application and knowledge
>
> knowledge of key sight words
>
> applied comprehension levels ... silent, oral, and listening
>
> from: Education Services, Inc.
>      8604 Baylor Circle
>      Orlando, Fla. 32817

*Classroom Reading Inventory* by Nicholas J. Silvaroli, which yields information such as:

> independent, instructional, and frustration levels
>
> specific word recognition and comprehension
>
> application of phonic knowledge
>
> level of listening comprehension
>
> level of phonetic application in spelling
>
> from: Wm. C. Brown Company Pub.
>      Dubuque, Iowa